Sandia Mountain Hiking Guide

Sandia Mountain Hiking Guide

MIKE COLTRIN

UNIVERSITY OF NEW MEXICO PRESS ▌▌ ALBUQUERQUE

10   09   08   07   06   05   2   3   4   5   6   7

Library of Congress Cataloging-in-Publication Data

Coltrin, Michael Elliott, 1953–
  Sandia Mountain hiking guide / Mike Coltrin.
     p. cm.
  Includes bibliographical references and index.
  ISBN 0-8263-3661-2 (spiral paperbound : alk. paper)
  1. Hiking—New Mexico—Sandia Mountains—Guidebooks.
2. Trails—New Mexico—Sandia Mountains—Guidebooks.
3. Sandia Mountains (N.M.)—Guidebooks.   I. Title.
  GV199.42.N62S263 2005
  917.89'504'54—dc22
                          2004024855

Photographs © Mike Coltrin, 2004
Maps © Barry L. Roberts and Mike Coltrin, 2004
Elevation profiles © Mike Coltrin, 2004

Design and type composition by Melissa Tandysh

Contents

List of Illustrations

Photos

Maps

To my fellow hiking enthusiasts:
May you find the peace and beauty in the
Sandia Mountains that I have enjoyed.

Preface

The Sandia Mountains furnish a wonderful natural resource at the edge of Albuquerque, New Mexico. Several times every day, I try to flee the confines of my office job and take a quick escape to the mountains, looking at them rising to the east. Better still is to go into the mountains and enjoy the scenery and serenity that they offer.

This guide describes hiking trails of the Sandia Mountains. Many Albuquerque residents have made the twisting trek up La Luz Trail at one time or another. To the majority of people, if you mention hiking in the Sandias that particular trail comes to mind. In fact the mountain is covered with hiking trails of all sorts, lengths, and difficulty. This book describes about sixty separate trails in the Sandia Mountains.

I have hiked all of the trails described in this book many times. I often make it a goal to take all of the hikes listed here within a single calendar year. When I got my new handheld Global Positioning System (GPS) and decided to record track information on all of the trails, I completed all of these hikes within a three-month period.

If there is a way to get disoriented or to lose a given trail in the Sandias, believe me I've done it. I have always kept a hiking diary to record any tricks for finding a certain trail, or landmarks to look for along the way, or how to find the spot where one trail crosses another. Some trails are hard to find. For example, I'm sure that I tried to find the Chimney Canyon Route a half-dozen times before I learned exactly how to do it. This book is meant to help all of us navigate the paths "off the beaten path."

I hope that you will enjoy the trails and the wide range of hiking opportunities in the Sandia Mountains as much as I have. If this guide opens up new outdoor experiences and appreciation for the wilderness "right next-door," then it will have done its job.

Acknowledgments

I would like to thank Dave Jackson for his support, advocacy, and encouragement in this project. Dave Jackson, Gerry Sussman, and Bob Julyan were all instrumental in bringing my writing to the attention of the University of New Mexico Press, which led to the production of this book. I am grateful to senior editor David Holtby of UNM Press for his help in seeing the project through to completion.

I am grateful for the collaboration of Barry Roberts, who designed and produced the high-quality topographic maps for this book. His knowledge of Geographic Information Systems (GIS) data formats and software options enabled us to create beautiful trail maps on a minimal budget.

Dave Holmes is a long-time hiker of the Sandia Mountains, whom I met on Peñasco Blanco Trail several years ago. He has covered all of the ground discussed here every year for the past forty years, or so. Dave has patiently described nooks and crannies all over the mountain and sent me off to find them. He has also given me many firsthand accounts of historical events related to the trails, old newspaper clippings, and beautiful old photographs of the mountain. I appreciate the knowledge that he has passed on to me and will try to preserve it.

I gratefully acknowledge Mike Hill, who wrote the predecessor to this hiking guide (see Appendix: Additional Reading). I first came to know and love the Sandia Mountains through reading his books.

Most of the trail-name origins that are mentioned in this guide were obtained from a compilation by Bob Julyan in the new *Field Guide to the Sandia Mountains* (see Additional Reading). I also appreciate Bob's advice on the content and revisions of this manuscript. I have benefited from his interest and experience.

I would like to thank Don Bush for providing information about the history of Peñasco Blanco Trail. I am also grateful to Sue B. Mann for her thoughtful and thorough editing of my manuscript.

Finally I would like to thank the many people who have read these descriptions, have gone out to take a hike, and then gave me feedback. It is a pleasure to hear other people's views of the Sandia Mountains.

General Information

Sandia Mountains

The Sandia Mountains prevail over the eastern skyline of Albuquerque, and they provide a constant point of reference and orientation for all who live nearby. They dominate the local weather patterns. The Sandias form a natural boundary for the city's eastern spread. They are simultaneously lush and arid, both wilderness and tourist destinations.

Rising to 10,678 feet at the Crest, with over 400 square miles in area, recreational opportunities abound in the Sandia Mountains. They offer cool relief from summer heat, fun play in winter snow, and places to enjoy stunning natural settings just minutes from the city's crowded streets.

In Tiwa, the language of Indians living in Isleta and Sandia pueblos, the mountain is called *Oku Pin* (Turtle Mountain); in the related Tewa tongue it is *Bien Mur* (Big Mountain). *Sandia* is the Spanish word for watermelon. The most popular explanation for the name origin comes from the pink hue that the granite face of the mountain acquires just at sunset, the color of watermelon. The actual name origin is probably less romantic. Spanish explorers visiting the Tiwa pueblo (now called Sandia) in the 1540s mistakenly believed that large gourds growing in the settlement were watermelons. The name was probably transferred to the pueblo and then to the mountains.

Life Zones

Four of the seven ecosystem life zones of North America can be found in the Sandia Mountains. Ascending in elevation from the base of the mountains to Sandia Crest is equivalent to a trip from the Sonoran Desert in

Mexico to the Hudson Bay in Canada. Only the Tropical and Lower Sonoran life zones (far southern latitudes) and the Alpine life zone (far north) are not represented in the Sandia Mountains.

The vegetation found between 6,000' and 7,500' elevation characterizes the Upper Sonoran Zone, which has hot summers, mild winters, and modest precipitation. This zone features cactus, chamisa, piñon-juniper forests, gray oak, cottonwood (near water), and box elder trees. The Transition life zone is found between about 7,500' and 8,200', with mild weather in the summer and cold winters, often with substantial snowfall. The ponderosa pine is dominant in this zone. Other common trees are the Gambel oak (scrub oak) and the piñon. Higher up the mountain, the Canadian zone is found between about 8,200' and 10,000', with cool summers, cold winters, and lots of moisture. Common trees found in this range include the Douglas fir, white fir, and aspen. Above about 10,000' is the Hudsonian life zone, in which summers are cool, winters are very cold, and snowfall is considerable. At these highest elevations, Engelmann spruce, white fir, and aspen are common.

Fig. 1. View of Sandia Crest from the south.

Geology

The Sandias were formed five to ten million years ago when a massive block of the earth's crust tilted up and sideways forming the craggy western face of the mountain. At one time the height of the western face was as much as twenty thousand feet. However, the far western face gradually broke away as the Rio Grande Valley dropped beneath it. The crumbled rock below the surface of the current riverbed accounts for the aquifer holding huge amounts of water beneath the river valley.

At the top of the Sandia Mountains, visible from the west, are alternating bands of shale and limestone formed from ocean sediments 250–300 million years ago. Below this is Precambrian granite formed 1.4 billion years ago from cooling magma. The huge face of the Shield, formed from this granite, dominates the northern profile of the mountain as viewed from most of Albuquerque. For additional information, see *Geology of the Sandia Mountains and Vicinity, New Mexico,* listed in Appendix 4: Additional Reading

Human Habitation

Early groups of people lived in Las Huertas Canyon in the northeastern portion of the Sandias ten thousand or more years ago. Artifacts from their presence were discovered in the Sandia Cave, excavated in the 1930s. The area was inhabited by groups of hunting people for thousands of years afterward. The lives of these natives eventually became more agriculture based, and groups of people began banding together, developing into the New Mexico Pueblo people. The mountain range remains a sacred place for the adjoining Sandia Pueblo. Spanish influence in the area began in the 1500s with expeditions in search of gold traveling up the Rio Grande Valley. The nearby city of Albuquerque has experienced rapid growth since World War II. Today Albuquerque, with a population of a half million, presses against the western foothills of the Sandias.

Administration

The Sandia Mountains form part of the Cibola National Forest, administered by the Sandia Ranger District. Main offices for the Cibola National Forest are located at 2113 Osuna Road NE, Suite A, Albuquerque, NM 87113–1001, phone (505) 346–3900.

The Ranger Station and offices for the Sandia Ranger District are on NM 337, one-half mile south of NM 333 (old Route 66), in Tijeras, NM, phone (505) 281–3304. The Ranger Station is a great source of information about the mountains, and I recommend visiting there. The U. S. Forest Service often sponsors wildflower walks on Saturday mornings, and other educational events. Contact the Sandia Ranger District for times and details.

Almost half of the mountain, 37,232 acres, was designated as the Sandia Mountain Wilderness Area in 1979. Special rules and conditions are in place to preserve the wilderness area in its natural state. By federal regulation, within the wilderness all wheeled mechanisms (except wheelchairs) including motorized equipment, mechanized equipment, bicycles, wagons, carts, and wheelbarrows are prohibited. Chainsaws are also prohibited. Permanent structures are not allowed, except for preexisting structures of historical value. No organized competitive events, such as footraces, can be held within the wilderness area. (An exception is made for the annual La Luz Trail race.) Boundaries of the wilderness area are generally marked with hand-tooled wooden signs, and are also designated on most maps of the area.

Animal Life

The Sandia Mountains are home to 58 different species of mammals, 34 species of reptiles, 6 species of amphibians, and 253 species of birds. The larger mammals include mule deer, black bear, bobcats, badgers, and porcupines. The population of bighorn sheep was once as high as one hundred in the 1950s, but it has been years since they were last seen in the Sandias. A few mountain lions still inhabit the Sandia Mountains; their population is hard to know, but is likely less than five.

Do not feed or leave food for the wildlife in the mountains. Doing so makes the animals associate human contact with an easy source of food, which will lead to inappropriate aggressive behavior and great problems. The harsh, but realistic, phrase from the U. S. National Park Service is "a fed animal is a dead animal."

Hiking in the Sandias

What to Take Along

Day pack

I always carry a day pack (small backpack) whenever I hike. When hiking to remote portions of the mountain, you need to be prepared for an unexpected overnight stay. A fall, broken bone, or other injury may prevent you from hiking out on your own. You need to be prepared to stay dry and warm in case you have to be out in the elements overnight until help arrives. The odds are that you will not have such an emergency. But unless you prepare for one, a bad situation could quickly escalate into a life threatening one.

Packing list

I have my day pack full of the items listed below. Although it seems like a lot of preparation, I just leave it packed from week to week, and know it is ready to go anytime that I head out the door. I carry extra articles of clothing, wrapped in plastic bags to keep them dry, including: a warm sweater, an extra pair of socks, a stocking cap, underwear, and a bandana. In plastic baggies, I carry other supplies, including: an LED flashlight, extra batteries, Band-Aids, matches, squares of newspaper, cigarette lighter, lip balm, a whistle, twine / strong cord, shoelaces, mole skin, and a small first-aid kit. In addition, I carry: a compass, sunscreen, a windbreaker, a mirror, pocket knife, rain poncho, a couple of plastic trash bags, and an extra set of car keys. Whew! I will probably never have to use most of these things, but I'd rather have it and not need it, than . . . (you know the rest).

Water

Always carry plenty of water on any hike. I always take at least a half gallon of water on any hike. I sometimes partially fill a water bottle and put it in the freezer the night before. I fill it the rest of the way with water right before leaving home, and have cold water for the whole hike.

There are many springs in the Sandia Mountains. However, you should not consider any water sources in the Sandia Mountains to be drinkable without appropriate mechanical filtration, chemical treatment, or boiling. Such springs often run dry, and generally cannot be relied upon as water sources.

Plan on carrying all of the water that you need for your hike in the Sandias. Back packers hiking the length of the Crest Trail often replenish with water at the Crest House or the upper Tram Terminal.

Food

I always carry a lunch or supply of snacks (and plenty of extras) to enjoy along the way. If you end up having to spend the night on a mountain, a supply of extra food will help keep up your energy.

Clothing

The standard advice is to dress in layers. Be sure that you have the clothes you need to keep warm. You can always peel off layers and stuff them in your day pack as you get warmer. Temperatures at the top of the mountain when the sun is waning might be twenty degrees cooler than when you started on a hike. So be prepared for a range of temperatures on any given day. I would recommend that you always wear a hat to protect your face and ears from the rays of the sun, as well as to keep your head cooler when it's hot, and warmer when it's cold.

Hiking boots

Although not strictly necessary, I would recommend hiking in a good pair of hiking boots. Many, if not most, of the trails can be rocky, uneven, and sometimes slick. Hiking boots will protect your feet and give you much better footing. Most importantly, a good pair of hiking boots will protect you from a turned ankle. You do not want to get five miles from the nearest trailhead and come up with a sprained ankle as the sun starts sinking in the sky.

Modern hiking socks are very good, particularly when used with thin socks next to your feet. Visit a sporting-goods store to purchase a nice pair of hiking socks, such as a blend of wool and modern polyester. Such socks provide warmth and cushioning, and are breathable to wick moisture away, keeping your feet dry.

Hike with a friend

I do not recommend hiking alone in the mountains. Not only will you enjoy the companionship and sharing the outdoor experience if you hike with a friend, but in case of emergency you (or your partner) can always go for help.

If you do choose to hike alone, you must make sure to tell someone else your hiking plans. Tell a friend the route that you plan to hike and the approximate time that you will return. At the minimum, leave this same information on the dashboard of your car as you park at the trailhead. As I was preparing this hiking guide, a solo hiker tragically died in the Sandia Mountains because no one knew that she was missing until several days after she had become lost.

Dogs

Many people enjoy bringing their dogs along while hiking in the Sandias. This can be good exercise for the family pet, and gives him an opportunity to enjoy the outdoors. However, you need to be responsible when taking your dog on a hike. Regulations require that dogs be on a leash at all times in the Sandia Mountains. Take along a plastic grocery sack to pack-out any droppings that your dog deposits along the way. Be sure to take extra water for your dog; he can become dehydrated even faster than you. Also, when hiking over rocky areas, be aware of the condition of the soft pads on your dog's paws.

Cell Phones

Taking a cell phone to the mountains is somewhat controversial these days. I believe that leaving the cell phone on, and taking calls from the family about soccer practice or what's for dinner will lessen your getaway experience. However, I am a realist and know that those calls can be important for many people. But, most importantly, I think that a cell phone might one day prove invaluable in an emergency or to summon help for a lost or injured hiker. If you have a cell phone, I say take it along for a safety backup. Cell-phone coverage in some places may be poor or nonexistent. Ridges generally provide better coverage than canyon bottoms. (See the section below, with the heading "If you get lost.")

Maps

A large topographic map is included with this book. It is important to learn to read this contour map, and always to have a good idea where you are on the mountain. I always keep a map in my day pack while hiking, and refer to it as I hike.

Parking Fees

There is a fee to park at most trailhead parking areas around the Sandia Mountains. The fee is currently three dollars per vehicle per day. If you plan to do much hiking, you can purchase a parking pass. The price (in 2004) is thirty dollars for a one-year pass. Persons with Golden Age Passports and Golden Eagle Passports may park at fee locations by leaving the card on the windshield or dashboard of their vehicle.

There is also a fee to park at the Elena Gallegos Picnic Area, run by the City of Albuquerque. The fee is one dollar on weekdays, and two dollars on weekends. An annual parking pass may be purchased for $26.40 (at the time of publication), if you plan on visiting this area often.

Hiking Safety

The main consideration when hiking in the mountains is safety. You should always be aware that you are entering a wilderness area. The mountains and the elements can be very unforgiving. You need to prepare accordingly.

Sun

Because of the high elevations, the sun shines hot and intense with Ultra Violet (UV) rays. Skin cancer is a very serious health risk for residents of New Mexico. Exposure to the sun in the middle of the day can quickly lead to painful sunburn. Be sure to protect your skin with a generous application of sunscreen while hiking. Sunscreen lotion wears off the skin from sweating and rubbing against clothes, so reapply every few hours on a long hike. UV radiation from the sun is most intense between about 10 A.M. and 3 P.M. In summer months, try to plan your hike for early in the morning to avoid the heat and intense sunshine of midday. (See also the discussion of Heat Exhaustion, below.) A broad-brimmed hat keeps the sun off your face, neck, and ears. Wearing long sleeves and pants protects you from the sun as well as scratches from low-lying trees and shrubs.

Snow

Be very cautious when hiking into snow. From November through April some portions of the mountain, especially upper La Luz Trail, are impassable because of snow coverage. Do not try to hike through deep snow (higher than your knee) when dressed in a light jacket, jeans, and tennis shoes. Incredibly, many people do, and run severe risk of hypothermia or even death. If you run into such snow and are unprepared for it, simply turn around and hike back to your car. (Hypothermia risks and first aid are also discussed below.)

When planning to hike in snow, the main considerations are keeping warm and dry. Dress in layers that can be added or removed to prevent overheating. Wear a warm cap (for example, a stocking cap) that can be pulled down over your ears and face, waterproof gloves or mittens, water-repellent trousers, and gaiters to keep snow out of your boots. Hiking in the snow can be fun and invigorating but also potentially dangerous.

Weather Patterns

Although the Albuquerque area is generally very dry, afternoon thunder-showers in the Sandia Mountains are quite common, especially during the

Fig. 2. Information signs near the Embudo trailhead.

monsoon season of July and August. Dangers from a sudden mountain storm include lightning, hail, flash flood, and hypothermia. Always take along rain gear when hiking in the Sandias. You can avoid most thunderstorms, as well as the afternoon heat, by planning your hikes for early in the day.

Lightning

New Mexico has the highest rate of deaths due to lightning per capita in the United States. The sound of a thunderclap from lightning takes about five seconds per mile to reach your ears. You can estimate how far away a lightning strike is by counting the time delay between the flash and the sound of thunder. Should you find yourself on the mountain in an approaching thunderstorm, take immediate precautions. Avoid high exposed places, such as ridges, or lone trees. Seek low, treeless areas and squat on two feet to present a low profile for lightning strikes. Do not seek shelter in a cave unless its depth is at least three times its opening distance. Take off your backpack and place it at least thirty feet away from yourself, to distance yourself from any metal or electronic gear that you may be carrying. Planning your hike for early in the day, before afternoon thundershowers typically arise, is the best way to avoid the potential dangers of lightning.

Flash Floods

Afternoon thunderstorms are usually short in duration, but can be quite intense. Should such conditions arise, stay clear of arroyos and steep, narrow canyons. Runoff from heavy rain draining into the narrow slot of a canyon can yield a flash flood with rapidly rising water and tremendous intensity. If you are caught in such a situation, immediately climb to higher ground, rather than vainly attempting to walk downstream ahead of the rising water. A flash flood can arise even when the sky overhead is dry and clear if a storm is raging farther above you on the mountain.

Rattlesnakes

There are rattlesnakes in the Sandia Mountains, the most common species being the Western Diamondback. Rattlesnakes are usually, but not always, found below eight thousand feet elevation. Rattlesnakes are most active at night, when it is cooler. For this reason, if you hike at night always use a flashlight (not only to spot a rattlesnake in your path, but also to avoid hazards such as rocks and drop-offs in the trail). You cannot depend on a rattlesnake to advertise its presence with its characteristic rattle sound, although most do.

To avoid a hiding rattlesnake, never reach into holes, crevices, or places you cannot see. Do not touch or attempt to move a rattlesnake if you encounter one. Seek immediate medical attention if bitten. Most wilderness guides recommend against attempting treatment for snakebite in the field.

Bears

Black bears are the only bear species in the Sandia Mountains. The bear population in the Sandias fluctuates, but is typically in the range of fifty to one hundred. I have seen bears many times on my hikes, usually within a few miles of Sandia Crest.

If you encounter a bear, it will most likely be frightened of you and run away. If you should see a bear before it sees you, make your presence known by speaking in a conversational tone of voice and slowly waving your arms. Both the sound and the action uniquely identify you as human (as opposed to some other animal), and the bear should run away. Avoid direct eye contact, which could be interpreted by the bear as a sign of aggression. In the extremely unlikely event that a black bear should attack you, fight back with all your might, using any objects that you can (hiking stick, rock, knife).

Never feed a bear (or other wildlife) in the mountains. Doing so will make the animal associate human contact with an easy source of food. The bear will begin to lose its fear of humans, which will ultimately lead to its death by game officials.

The Sandia Mountain Bear Watch is an organization to educate people on how to live with wildlife and to protect the black bear in New Mexico. For more information contact Jan Hayes, P.O. Box 591, Tijeras, NM 87059, phone (505) 281–9282.

Poison Ivy

Poison ivy is common in damp areas along trails in the Sandia Mountains. The best defense against poison ivy is learning to identify the plant by its shiny green leaves in groups of three, and avoiding contact. Long pants and sleeves protect skin from direct contact with poison ivy. However, the oil (*urushiol*) from the plant can cling to clothes and can still cause a rash upon later exposure to the skin. Wash your skin with soap and water if exposed to poison ivy, and all clothing if you may have walked through it. If a rash develops, over-the-counter medications will usually suffice.

Plague

Visitors might be surprised to learn that fleas carrying bubonic plague can sometimes be found in New Mexico. Stay away from any dead rodents that you might come across while in the wilderness. When hiking with a dog, it might be tempted to investigate a dead rodent encountered along the way. Fleas carrying plague could easily be transferred to your pet (and then to you), so keep dogs away from this potential hazard.

Heat exhaustion

Overexertion in the New Mexico sun can lead to heat exhaustion or even heat stroke. Common-sense precautions will go a long way toward avoiding this situation. These include planning your hike for early morning during the summer, dressing in lightweight clothing, wearing a hat to shield your face and head from the sun, and drinking plenty of water along the way. Signs of heat exhaustion include dizziness or lightheadedness, confusion, nausea, and a quickened pulse. Should these signs occur, have the victim lie down in the shade, apply a damp cloth to their face and upper body, and have the victim slowly drink water.

Hypothermia

Hypothermia is the condition of abnormally low body temperature. More people actually die of hypothermia during summer than winter. However, proper preparation should make your risk very low. The main causes of hypothermia are cold, wind, and wetness. Prepare for the worst weather possible. Bring complete body protection, and put it on before becoming cold. Eat snacks along your hike, which provide your body with quickly accessible energy supplies. The signs of hypothermia include shivering, mental confusion, sluggishness or drowsiness, cold skin, and slowed breathing or heart rate. Should these signs occur, shelter the victim from the cold and wind, cover their head and neck, and insulate them from the cold ground. If the victim is alert and can easily swallow, give them warm, sweetened fluids.

Altitude

For people who live in Albuquerque, altitude sickness should not be a problem when hiking in the Sandia Mountains. However, visitors from places with lower elevations would be advised to wait a few days before hiking in the Sandias to partially acclimate to the altitude. Albuquerque and the base of the mountains are over five thousand feet in elevation. Visitors should wait at least two days at the intermediate elevations of Albuquerque before attempting a hike that ventures to nine thousand feet elevation, or higher.

If You Get Lost

It is unlikely that you will get really lost in the Sandia Mountains. However, it is easy to wander off some of the lesser used trails. As you are hiking it is always a good idea to make sure you stay on the main trail. There are numerous "volunteer paths" and game trails crisscrossing the trails described here, and it is easy to walk off the trail and end up at an obvious dead end. If this should happen, try to retrace your steps until you are sure that you have returned to the original trail that you intended.

Cell phones can be very helpful in an emergency. The Forest Service, State Police, and Sheriff's office recommend that you call 911 and be prepared to give the following information: (a) your name, (b) what is wrong (injury, lost, physical condition, etc.), (c) your approximate location (all trails on the west side of the mountain are *not* the La Luz Trail; you should know the name of the trail that you are hiking), (d) your cell phone number. If you have a GPS, take a reading and give the coordinates to the 911 Operator. This will help the Search and Rescue to find you faster. Importantly, save your cell-phone batteries so that Search and Rescue can call you. For example, do not call a list of your friends to tell them your problems, draining the phone batteries but not helping your situation.

Search and Rescue is coordinated statewide by the New Mexico State Police. Most rescue-team participants are highly trained and well-equipped volunteers, so it can take some time for them to get organized and start the rescue effort. Be patient, help is coming.

If you come across someone who needs assistance, help them. It is best not to leave an injured person by themselves, but to send someone to get help.

If you are lost, stay in one place; you will be easier to find if you are not wandering around. Although you may be able to see Albuquerque from the west side of the mountain, don't try to walk down a canyon. Some canyons are impassable.

Always let someone know where you are going to hike and when you expect to return so that authorities can be notified if you have a problem and don't return home. If you can't do that, leave a note on your car dashboard that will give information to people who may need to search for you.

Help Preserve the Mountains

Leave No Trace

"Take only photographs, and leave only footprints."

Minimize your impact on the mountain environment. This ethic is popularly summarized as "Leave No Trace." For detailed guidelines, consult the U.S. Forest Service brochure by that name, or the book titled *Leave No Trace* listed in Appendix 4: Additional Reading.

Be a good citizen of the mountains, and leave them as beautiful as you found them. This includes packing out all trash, cans, food, and paper that you have brought into the wilderness. Do not take shortcuts across

Fig. 3. Trail leading to South Sandia Peak from the south.

switchbacks, which causes erosion to the trails. Please don't pick wild-flowers, cactus, or other vegetation.

Stay on established trails whenever possible, walking single file. Obey posted Trail Closure signs.

Dispose of all human waste in a "cat hole" six to eight inches deep. Cover and disguise when you are finished. Stay well away from trails and at least two hundred feet away from any stream or drainage. Toilet paper should be packed out (not buried or burned) in a sealed plastic bag.

Do not throw or push over rocks from the trails. Someone could be below you without your knowing it, turning a prank into a dangerous injury.

Trail Manners
Livestock and people with small children always have the right-of-way, as do mountain bikes. Hikers have more control and can get out of the way more easily than either horses or bike riders. It is not legal to operate mountain bikes or any other wheeled or powered vehicle (or machine) within the Sandia Mountain Wilderness. (See the Mountain Biking section below for more details.)

Trail Closures
At certain times of the year some trails may be closed to protect sensitive vegetation, wildlife, or migrating birds. Specifically, the area east of Piedra Lisa Trail is closed off every year from March 1 to August 15 to protect sensitive wildlife areas. Usually signs posted at trailheads give notice of closings. Failure to observe these closures can result in a significant fine.

Fire Danger
In years of low rainfall, which have been coming more often lately, fire restrictions may be in place. Often this means that no open fires can be started within the Sandia Mountain district. All access to hiking trails may be shut off in times of extreme fire danger. Please obey all such fire warnings and closures.

Enjoying the Sandias
Picnic Areas
There are numerous picnic areas around the Sandia Mountains, with hours of operation from 6 A.M. to 10 P.M. All picnic areas have grills, tables,

and restroom facilities. Bring your own wood for fires. Most picnic grounds are open from May 1 through November 1. Use of picnic grounds in the Sandia Mountains by groups is by reservation only through the Sandia Ranger District Office at (505) 281–3304. Group fees for picnic areas with shelters were sixty dollars (Friday-Sunday) and forty dollars (Monday-Thursday) in 2003. Contact the Sandia Ranger District for a complete list of picnic areas and details.

Mountain Biking

Bicycles are prohibited within the areas designated as Sandia Mountain Wilderness. However, mountain biking is allowed on a number of the trails outside the Sandia Wilderness boundaries. There is a nice system of bike trails in the western foothills, convenient to Albuquerque. Cedro Peak, south of Interstate 40, is covered with mountain bike trails; maps are available at bike shops and sporting-goods stores. Biking in the Sandia Peak Ski Area is open on weekends and holidays from Memorial Day through Labor Day. A bike shop at the site offers rental packages. You and your bike may take the chairlift up the mountain, and then mountain bike down. Helmets are mandatory.

Hiking trails on which biking is allowed include: Tree Spring Trail, 10K Trail (except the portion northwest of Ellis Trail), Bill Spring Trail, Rozamiento Trail, Foothills Trail, Boundary Loop Route, Strip Mine Trail, Ellis Trail (south of the junction with 10K Trail), and Faulty Trail (north of the junction with Bart's Trail). Local mountain biking guides are listed in the Additional Reading section in Appendix 4.

Backpacking

Backpacking and overnight camping are allowed within the Sandia Mountains. Permits are not required. The most popular route for back-packers is probably the Crest Trail, stretching twenty-six miles along a north-south corridor. Beautiful and remote areas for hiking and camping are available along this trail. Please camp at least two hundred feet from streambeds. Choose a campsite that has been used before if you are in a well-traveled area, which will likely be the case. This will limit the spread of human impact on the mountain. Try to use a camp stove and lantern to avoid a campfire and accompanying blackened earth. Water availability is extremely limited within the Sandias, so unless you have recent first-hand information that a spring is running, plan to carry all the water you need. As mentioned below, no spring water in the Sandia Mountains should be considered drinkable without boiling, chemical, or mechanical treatment. Backpackers traversing the Crest Trail often refill their water supply at the Upper Tram Terminal.

Sandia Peak Ski Area

The Sandia Peak Ski Area offers downhill skiing on thirty trails serviced by four chairlifts. The ski season is approximately December through March. The ski area includes a certified ski school, rental shop, café, and outdoor grill. Skiers can either drive to the base of the ski area about five miles up the Crest Highway, or ride the Sandia Peak Aerial Tramway (reduced fares for the Tramway ride are offered when purchasing a lift ticket). Contact the Sandia Peak Ski Area at (505) 242–9133 for more information.

Cross-Country Skiing

Cross-country ski touring is available near Sandia Crest in the winter months. Several of the hiking trails mentioned in this guide are used as cross-country ski trails in the winter. They include the Crest Trail, Ellis Trail, 10K Trail, and Tree Spring Trail, as well as many other trails between the Crest Highway and the Upper Tram Terminal, and the Capulin Peak area. A map entitled "Cross Country Ski Touring Map" is available from the Sandia Ranger District and at sporting-goods stores. A cross-country trail guide is listed in Appendix 4: Additional Reading.

Capulin Snow Play Area

The Capulin Snow Play Area is usually open from December to March. The area is available for inner tubing and riding on soft sliding devices. Skis, sleds (with wood, metal, or other hard material), and snowboards are prohibited. The Snow Play Area is usually open Friday through Sunday from 9:30 A.M. to 4 P.M. and everyday during the weeks before and after Christmas. Note that sledding, tubing, and sliding are prohibited at the 10K Trail and Tree Spring trailhead areas.

Hunting

Firearms are not allowed within the Sandia Mountain Wilderness. There is a limited deer hunt most years for bow hunters. Contact the New Mexico Department of Game and Fish, P. O. Box 25112, Santa Fe, NM

87507, phone (800)–862–9310, for information about dates, restrictions, and licenses.

Open Space

Open Space is undeveloped land set aside for conservation and/or passive recreation. The City of Albuquerque has made a significant investment in Open Space areas. In particular, two large Open Space areas lie at the western foothills of the Sandia Mountains. The first is the 640-acre Elena Gallegos/Albert G. Simms Park, which is east of Tramway Blvd. and roughly midway between the Sandia Peak Aerial Tramway and Montgomery Blvd. The area has numerous hiking and biking trails and picnic facilities. The Foothills Open Space covers a 1,200 acre strip of land running along the western foothills, with numerous trailheads between Copper and Montgomery Blvds. For more information contact the City of Albuquerque, Parks and Recreation Department, Open Space Division, P. O. Box 1293, Albuquerque, NM 87103, phone (505) 452–5200.

Bernalillo County also has an Open Space program, with two significant areas at the southern end of the Sandia Mountains. A 450-acre parcel of land in Three Gun Spring Canyon north of the Monticello Neighborhood was jointly purchased by the U. S. Forest Service, Bernalillo County, and the City of Albuquerque. The property was purchased to protect the area from future housing development and to ensure access to Cibola National Forest lands. The second property is Carlito Springs, just west of Canyon Estates and north of I-40. Over the years, this beautiful 177-acre area has been used as a stagecoach shop, a boy's home, a tuberculosis sanatorium, and a family residence. In 2004, the property was being renovated and plans for public access were being formulated. For more information contact the Open Space Coordinator, Bernalillo County Parks and Recreation, 2400 Broadway SE, Albuquerque, NM 87102, phone (505) 842–7110.

Hiking Clubs

A number of hiking organizations and clubs sponsor organized hikes and outdoor-awareness programs. The largest organization is the New Mexico Mountain Club, founded in 1952, with over one thousand members. They offer a variety of hikes around the state and in the Sandia Mountains. Monthly meetings are held on the third Wednesday of every month at Congregation B'Nai Israel, 4401 Indian School Rd. NE, in Albuquerque.

Contact the New Mexico Mountain Club, P. O. Box 4151, University Station, Albuquerque, NM 87196 for more information.

How to Use This Guide

This book describes about sixty trails in the Sandia Mountains. Accompanying each trail description is the length of the trail (most are one-way distances), the elevation range that you will cover, a Difficulty Rating (easy, moderate, difficult, or most difficult), the map number (and page) of the single-page topographic map highlighting the trail, and detailed driving instructions. For trails with significant elevation change (over 350 feet), there is also a chart of altitude that you will encounter versus distance along the hike. If weather either the heat of summer or the snow cover of winter—is a significant issue in hiking the trail, this is mentioned in the hike description.

The twenty-five topographical maps throughout the book show trails in different sections of the mountain. Elevation contours are drawn at 100' intervals (major contours are labeled every 500'). The distance scale varies from map to map, but a scale bar is always included. Coverage of the Crest Trail, Faulty Trail, and the Foothills Trail is split over several maps due to their great length.

Global Positioning System (GPS) information is referred to extensively in the book. You do not have to have a GPS to use this book, or to hike the trails described here. However, if you do have one of these position-finding systems, they can help you navigate along the way and in some cases find landmarks or forks in trails that may seem ambiguous in a written description.

Locations are usually referred to in the book in terms of GPS "waypoints," which are the actual coordinates (latitude and longitude) of points of interest. For example, in the hike description you might read: "Tree Spring Trail passes the intersection with Oso Corredor Trail (wp OSOTSP) about a third of a mile from the trailhead." The location of this intersection is referred to by the waypoint "name" OSOTSP rather than cluttering up the hike description with a lot of numbers (e.g., N 35° 11.524', W 106° 24.501'). The names are limited to six letters in many GPS units, and I've tried to make the short names descriptive. So how do you find out the actual latitude and longitude of these waypoint names that are referred to throughout the text? There is an Appendix at the end of the

Fig. 4. Elena Gallegos Open Space.

book with the complete list of over three hundred waypoints. These coordinates may be entered into your GPS unit to take with you on the hike, if you like. These waypoints are also included on the accompanying topographic maps throughout the book, to help associate the descriptions in the text with positions on the map.

There are several different settings on a GPS unit that affect the exact location reading that will be displayed. In this book, the latitude and longitude are listed in ddd° mm.mmm' format; see the previous paragraph for an example. (The same position in the so-called ddd.ddddd format would be N 35.19207°, W 106.40835°, so it does make a difference. Check the settings on your GPS unit.) The next important setting is the "map datum." The locations given in this book are based on the "WGS 84" datum. Make sure that your unit is configured to use this reference datum, or else the position you read may differ from the ones given here by one hundred feet, or more. Other settings for your GPS receiver include the units used for distance and elevation measurements (feet and miles, for example, versus metric) and heading (true north versus magnetic north). I cite all distances using the statute system of feet and miles, and reference to true north.

The trails in this book are divided into two large groups. The first set includes the most popular and well-established trails. These trails are generally maintained by the Forest Service, and include an official trail number. After that is a group called "Other Hiking Routes." These are generally easy to follow hiking areas that are not officially recognized by the Forest Service, but nonetheless are nice hiking destinations. The actual order of presentation of the main trails is by the location of the suggested trailhead (parking area) and driving route. The hike descriptions begin with trails from the bottom of the Crest Highway, and make a counterclockwise loop around the entire mountain range. The loop travels up the Crest Highway, then north through Las Huertas Canyon toward Placitas, then west toward I-25, then south along the western face of the Sandias toward Tijeras Canyon, then east through the canyon, and finally, north along the eastern foothills.

At the end of most trail descriptions is a short section called "Extending Your Hike." Here I give suggestions on combining a given trail with other trails in the area to form longer hikes and interesting loops.

A summary of all the hikes (distance, elevation range, and difficulty) is given on page 163, to help select a hike. An Appendix on page 165 also lists the trails sorted by Difficulty Rating.

Trail Descriptions

Cienega Trail (No. 148)

Length: 2.2 miles (one way)
Elevation: 7,500–9,220 feet
Rating: Moderate
See Map: 1 (page 26)
Driving Instructions: Take I-40 east from Albuquerque, go north on NM 14 for about six miles, and take the turnoff to the Crest Highway, NM 536. Drive 1.7 miles to the Sulphur Canyon Picnic Ground entrance. Make an immediate left turn on the asphalt road going up the hill; after one half mile, the road makes a "T" at a large parking area. Turn right and continue up the asphalt road one mile to the Cienega Trail parking area at the end of the road. Note: The road to the Cienega trailhead is closed during the winter months.

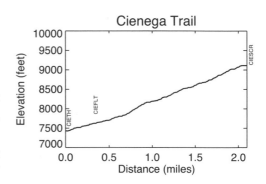

Description

Cienega Canyon is a beautiful area for a picnic, whether or not you are hiking. *Cienega* is Spanish for "wet meadow." As you are driving up the road, one-half mile past the "T" mentioned above, there is such a wet grassy meadow on your right. (The Cienega Nature Trail, a short 0.2 mile paved loop, is just north of this meadow.)

To find Cienega Trail (No. 148), walk west on the paved path from final parking area at the end of the road (wp CIETH). After a couple of hundred feet you will come to a trail sign, and see a large Forest Service trail map, marking the start of the Cienega Trail proper. A few hundred feet past the trailhead, Cienega Trail meanders along a beautiful streambed. The short hike to the source of this stream is popular with families who have young children.

After 0.4 miles Cienega Trail intersects Faulty Trail (wp CIEFLT), and you will enter a beautiful area with grass, streams, and high trees to the source of the stream. The trail is a steady climb uphill above this section and follows the streambed most of the way. Cienega Trail eventually becomes rocky and more sparsely vegetated. However, near the top the area turns more lush and pleasant. The trail terminates at the ridge, intersecting with Crest Trail (wp CIESCR). Pino Trail, coming up from the west side, also terminates here at the ridge.

For the best view, walk a few feet west up the limestone rock at the Cienega–Crest Trail junction, then take a faint path south, between the brush and the Crest Trail. After about one hundred feet look for a path to the west, which leads to an open, rocky limestone area (wp CIEOVL). There are lots of flat rocks to sit on and enjoy the views of Pino Canyon and Albuquerque to the west.

From here, either reverse your steps down Cienega Trail to your car, or explore areas of the Crest Trail to the north or to the south.

Extending your hike: You can make this hike into a nice, but long loop (eleven miles total) by continuing north on the Crest Trail, then hiking down Tree Spring Trail to Oso Corredor Trail, then making your way home on Oso Corredor Trail to Faulty Trail and back to Cienega Trail.

An alternate loop travels south on the Crest Trail to Cañoncito Trail, hiking down Cañoncito to Faulty Trail. Hike north on Faulty Trail to Cienega Canyon to close the hike, with a total distance of around 8.5 miles.

Armijo Trail (No. 222)

Length: 2.2 miles (one way)
Elevation: 7,100–7,230 feet
Rating: Moderate
Map: 1 (page 26)
Driving Instructions: Take I-40 east from Albuquerque, then go north on NM 14 for six miles, and take the turnoff to the Crest Highway (NM 536). Drive 1.7 miles to the Sulphur Canyon Picnic Ground entrance. Make an immediate left turn on the asphalt road going uphill; after one half mile, the road makes a "T" at a parking area, where you may leave your car (wp ARMPRK). Note: This asphalt road is closed during the winter; you may alternately park in the lot immediately to your right as you turn into the Sulphur Canyon area from the Crest Highway (wp SULPK). Doing so adds about one mile to your hike.

Description

Armijo Trail measures about two miles in length, with a modest elevation gain. It is one of the best-kept secrets in the Sandias and is a nice route through the green lower east side of the mountain. The path may be snow covered in the winter, but it should be hikeable all year round.

From the parking area (wp ARMPRK), walk east along the asphalt road blocked by several low posts. After about a quarter of a mile you pass an old picnic area on your left. Be sure to notice the unique stonework along the side of the road. Just past this, the road makes a small loop (wp ARMWP1). At the far end of the loop is a sign for the Cienega Horse Bypass branching off to the left and Armijo / Faulty Trail to the right. Take the right fork, and continue down the dirt path for 150 yards toward a fence (and private property). Just before the fence, another sign post points the way to a distinct trail going over a small ridge to the right. At the top of the ridge (only about twenty feet up), you will see a well-worn trail leading down into a valley and off to the southwest.

Armijo Trail is easy to follow, with only a slight uphill grade until it drops a short distance down into Armijo Canyon bottom after about a half mile. The hike is pleasant through ponderosa pine forest. In many places the trail runs parallel to a small intermittent stream. Follow Armijo Trail to its intersection with Faulty Trail (wp ARMFLT), marked by a sign. This marks the end of Armijo Trail. To return to your car, either retrace your steps or extend your hike as described below.

Extending your hike: Torro Spring (wp TORRSP) lies 0.2 mile up Armijo Canyon from the junction with Faulty Trail (wp ARMFLT). From the trail junction, head west and up the clearing that follows an old road. The road becomes a path and soon drops into the canyon bottom just to the south. Follow the canyon bottom about three hundred yards to find the deep spring. During a wet year, the spring may be five feet in diameter and five feet deep. The travertine rock formations around the spring are among the prettiest in the Sandias.

(**Note**: the last portion of the following route, past FLTWP2, may be snowy and treacherous in the winter. Please beware.) To make this hike into a nice loop, begin hiking north on Faulty Trail from the junction with Armijo Trail. After a mile you will reach a beautiful, high overlook above Cienega Canyon (wp FLTWP2). Faulty Trail then heads down a steep section of trail into the canyon, to the intersection with Cienega Trail (wp CIEFLT), marked by a sign. Take Cienega Trail east to complete the loop on this hike. It is a 0.4 mile walk to the Cienega trailhead. Follow the asphalt road downhill to reach the parking area (wp ARMPRK).

Fig. 5. Lush forest along Armijo Trail.

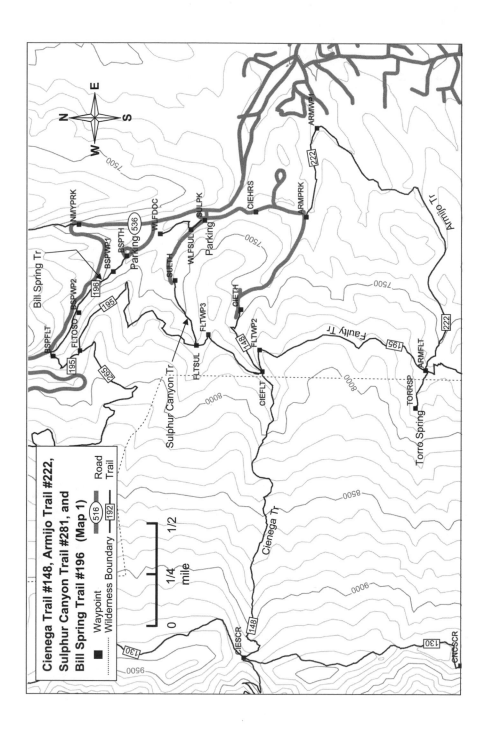

Cienega Trail #148, Armijo Trail #222,
Sulphur Canyon Trail #281, and
Bill Spring Trail #196 (Map 1)

Waypoint
Wilderness Boundary
516 Road
192 Trail

0   1/4   1/2
mile

Sulphur Canyon Trail (No. 281)

Length: 0.4 mile (one way)
Elevation: 7,420–7,620 feet
Rating: Easy
See Map: 1 (page 26)
Driving Instructions: Take I-40 east from Albuquerque, then go north on NM 14 for six miles, and take the turnoff to the Crest Highway (NM 536). Drive 1.7 miles to the Sulphur Canyon Picnic Ground, which is immediately to your right after you exit the Crest Highway.

Description

The trailhead for Sulphur Canyon Trail lies at the far end of the picnic area. During the winter the road past the first small parking area (wp SULPK) may be blocked by a metal gate. Just beyond this metal gate is Sulphur Spring itself (wp SULSPR) behind a fence on your right. The origin of the name of the spring and canyon is uncertain, but it may be related to an old nearby mine.

Continuing northwest (either driving or walking) along the asphalt road through the picnic area, you will reach a barricade blocking automobile traffic. The Sulphur Canyon trailhead is 0.15 mile past this barricade at a loop in the old asphalt road (wp SULTH). The trail begins with a gentle uphill grade through an area of red soil. It travels west through a 20'-wide grassy clearing, with thick overhead tree coverage in places. Sulphur Canyon Trail is outside the Sandia Mountain Wilderness area and receives a lot of mountain-bike traffic. If you encounter a cyclist yield the right-of-way and the trail to them.

Sulphur Canyon Trail terminates at its junction with Faulty Trail (wp FLTSUL). A small intermittent spring, Wolf Spring, is up the canyon just a bit west of this point.

Extending your hike: You can make a nice loop hike by continuing north on Faulty Trail, past its junction with Oso Corredor Trail, to join the Bill Spring Trail (wp BSPFLT). Bill Spring Trail will take you back to the Doc Long Picnic Ground. The short Wolf Creek Trail, marked by a sign just west of the main picnic pavilion, connects the Doc Long area (wp WLFDOC) to the Sulphur Canyon Picnic Ground (wp WLFSUL).

Alternately, from the west end of Sulphur Canyon Trail you can go south on Faulty Trail to make a loop with Cienega Trail (wp CIEFLT), hiking east through the Cienega Canyon Picnic Ground, and back to your car on the asphalt roads. For a somewhat longer loop, hike south on Faulty Trail to Armijo Trail (wp ARMFLT) and follow that trail east and north through the Cienega Canyon Picnic Ground to make your way back to your car.

Bill Spring Trail (No. 196)

Length: 0.7 mile (one way)
Elevation: 7,400–7,720 feet
Rating: Easy
See Map: 1 (page 26)
Driving Instructions: Take I-40 east from Albuquerque, then go north on NM 14 for six miles. Take the turnoff to the Crest Highway (NM 536), drive two miles, then turn into the Doc Long Picnic Ground. Follow the asphalt road past some large picnic pavilions, restroom facilities, and information signs, and park at the end of the pavement. In the winter, the first metal gate may be locked, so park there and walk to the end of the pavement.

Description
Bill Spring Trail starts from the northwest end of the Doc Long Picnic Ground. Workers from the Civilian Conservation Corps (CCC) built one of the large group picnic shelters in the 1930s. The picnic area is named for William H. "Doc" Long, one of the nation's first botanical researchers. In the early 1900s Long conducted research into diseases of forest trees and fruit in the Southwest United States. He arrived in Albuquerque in 1913 and established his field headquarters at this site. Doc Long did important work toward understanding diseases affecting ponderosa pines, such as dwarf mistletoe and tree rot. Bill Spring is most likely named after William (Doc) Long.

Bill Spring Trail is a beautiful short trail on the green lower east side of the Sandias. The trail, outside the Sandia Mountain Wilderness, is used by mountain bikers, hikers, and sometimes by cross-country skiers after a good snowfall. The trail maintains a modest elevation grade its entire length. Bill Spring Trail is shaded by thick tree cover, including ponderosa pine and Gambel oak, making a pleasant hike year round. The trail travels up Tejano Canyon (*Tejano* is Spanish for "Texan"), and lies just below the Crest Highway.

At the far end of the picnic area, the road terminates in a loop. To find the trailhead, take the asphalt path west of the picnic tables and follow it northwest for one hundred yards. At the end of the pavement, a sign marks the beginning of Bill Spring Trail and access to Faulty Trail, Oso Corredor Trail, and Sulphur Canyon. Bill Spring Trail begins as a wide rocky path, which was probably a road at one time.

After a quarter of a mile, the trail passes a water holding tank behind a chain-link fence and a wooden maintenance station. A faint trail crosses Bill Spring Trail at this point (wp BSPWP1); see the section Extending Your Hike for more information. Also, to the right of the trail is a small intermittent stream coming up from several 2'-diameter rocks in the streambed.

The trail passes by some large uptilting limestone formations about 0.4 miles into your walk. These impressive rocks look like they are pointing up toward Sandia Crest, and they are! A three-hundred-foot-thick series of limestone bands covered the area around 300 million years ago. When the Sandia Mountains were formed five to ten million years ago, a great slab of granite was pushed up, creating the steep western face of the mountains. The upslope "hinged" at the bottom east side of the current-day mountain range. Along Bill Spring Trail you see the same bands of limestone at around 7,500' elevation that are visible from Albuquerque below Sandia Crest (at an elevation of 10,500').

Bill Spring Trail soon crosses to the right side of the streambed, and about one hundred yards later (wp BSPWP2) passes the intermittent Bill Spring. The trail terminates about a quarter of a mile farther at the northern trailhead of Faulty Trail, marked by a sign and a wooden fence (wp BSPFLT).

Extending your hike: By continuing up Faulty Trail you have access to lots of nice hiking opportunities. After 0.2 mile on Faulty Trail you reach the junction with Oso Corredor Trail, which travels 2.7 miles to Tree Spring Trail. Or, continuing south on Faulty Trail for another mile, you can take Sulphur Canyon Trail back toward your car, forming a nice loop.

As mentioned above, a faint trail crosses Bill Spring Trail at the pumping shed (wp BSPWP1). This is the renegade North Mystery Trail, which runs from the junction of Faulty Trail and Sulphur Canyon Trail to Lagunita Seca (below Palomas Peak), a distance of about seven miles. The portion of North Mystery Trail crossing Bill Spring Trail and the streambed takes you northeast to the remnants of the old Crest Highway, which is fun to explore.

Faulty Trail (No. 195)

Length: 8.7 miles (one way)
Elevation: 7,000–7,860 feet
Rating: Moderate
See Maps (north to south coverage):
1 (page 26); 18 (page 118);
17 (page 114)
Driving Instructions: Take I-40 east from Albuquerque, then go north on NM 14 for six miles. Take the turnoff to the Crest Highway (NM 536) and

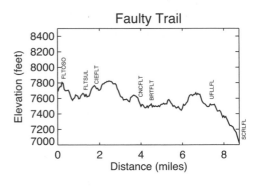

drive two miles to the Doc Long Picnic Ground. Follow the asphalt road past some large picnic pavilions, restroom facilities, and information signs, and park at the end of the pavement.

Description

Faulty Trail is an important north-south trail spanning nearly the entire distance from the Crest Highway to Interstate 40. It is a "connector" trail internal to the mountain, meaning that you must hike other trails to reach it. Faulty Trail intersects six major trails (Bill Spring, Sulphur Canyon, Cienega, Cañoncito, Bart's, and the Crest trails) near their lower trailheads, so easy access to Faulty Trail is available all along its length. This is important because any number of hiking combinations can be planned by using segments of Faulty Trail to link other trails together. There is relatively little elevation change over the 8.7-mile length of Faulty Trail (until the

600-foot difference between its junctions with Upper Faulty Trail and the Crest Trail). Faulty Trail to the north of Bart's Trail is outside the Sandia Mountain Wilderness, so mountain biking is allowed on that segment.

Faulty Trail was surreptitiously cleared by unknown persons during the 1970s and 1980s. These "trail blazers" marked the trail with distinctive diamond symbols carved into trees along the path. The trail came to be known by some as the Diamond Trail for the blaze marks, and by others as the Mystery Trail because of its unknown origins. The Forest Service eventually adopted the trail into the official system as the Faulty Trail. The southern portion of the trail roughly follows the geological Flatirons Fault of the mountain.

The northern trailhead for Faulty Trail is at the northwest end of Bill Spring Trail. (The driving directions above are for the Bill Spring trailhead. Because Faulty Trail crosses many other east-west trails, any of them can also be used for access farther south.) The hike up Bill Spring Trail to the Faulty trailhead is about 0.7 mile. Faulty Trail begins a steep 0.25-mile climb to meet the southeast trailhead of Oso Corredor Trail (wp FLTOSO). Faulty Trail then follows a contour toward the south, and it comes to the western terminus of the Sulphur Canyon Trail (wp FLTSUL) 1.2 miles farther.

The unofficial North Mystery Trail also joins Faulty and Sulphur Canyon Trails at this point. (See the description of North Mystery Trail later in this book.)

Continuing south, Faulty Trail enters Cienega Canyon and soon crosses Cienega Trail (wp CIEFLT). Immediately past the Cienega Trail junction, Faulty Trail makes a steep climb up the north-facing slope of the canyon. Be warned that this short segment of trail can be icy and treacherous in the winter. There is a beautiful view of the canyon from the rocky overlook at the top of this short climb (wp FLTWP2). The trail continues to the south through a piñon-juniper forest and reaches a junction with the Armijo Trail (wp ARMFLT) one mile later.

One mile to the south, Faulty Trail nears Cañoncito Spring. There is a remarkable tree (wp FLTTHG) next to Faulty Trail, just one hundred yards before the junction with Cañoncito Trail. This piñon tree has two distinct ninety-degree bends in its trunk; the tree trunk goes vertically from the ground for about five feet, then makes a bend to run horizontal for several feet, and then bends up and grows vertically. I had noted this tree a dozen times before I learned that it is called a "thong tree." The turns in the trunk are a manmade "road-sign." Native Americans often used leather straps or other devices to force a sapling to bend horizontally in a certain direction. The unstrapped end of the trunk would then turn to grow upward. Eventually the strap thong would break, with the bend in the tree remaining. Thong trees point to important landmarks, such as water, medicinal plants, or caves. This one points toward Cañoncito Spring just down the hill. (There is another thong tree, this one a ponderosa pine, about fifteen feet east of Faulty Trail in the first canyon south of Bart's Trail.)

Faulty Trail intersects Cañoncito Trail (wp CNCFLT) about fifty yards west of Cañoncito Spring. This delightful area features one of the most reliable springs in the Sandia Mountains. Usually water flows down a series of beautiful travertine falls within a few hundred yards downhill from the spring. It is well worth a side trip to visit this area.

About one half mile to the south, Faulty Trail crosses Bart's Trail (wp BRTFLT). Bart's Trail enters the Sandia Mountain Wilderness at this junction and heads steeply to the main ridgeline at the Crest Trail. A trail leading to the Cole Spring Picnic is passed 0.6 mile farther south (wp COLFLT).

Faulty Trail goes over a saddle point (wp REDSDL) 1.75 miles farther south, to the west of a hill that I call Red Hill because of the red dirt. This spot is one quarter mile north of the junction of Upper and Lower Faulty Trails. In 2003, a one-acre fire occurred just north of the saddle point, and Faulty Trail forms the west firebreak. It should be interesting to watch the natural recovery of the area as the forest heals itself over the coming years.

Faulty Trail splits at the Casa Loma saddle point (wp UFLLFL). South of this point, the main fork of the trail going south is referred to as Lower Faulty Trail. It continues 1.25 miles to terminate at the Crest Trail (wp SCRLFL); that junction is about 1 mile from the Crest Trail parking area at Canyon Estates. Lower Faulty Trail is marked with diamond blazes as is the northern trail. The most significant elevation grade along Faulty Trail is encountered just north of the Crest Trail junction.

From the Casa Loma saddle, the Upper Faulty Trail branches to the southwest. Upper Faulty follows a contour for 1.25 miles to join the Crest Trail (wp SCRUFL). That junction occurs about one mile farther up the Crest Trail from its junction with Lower Faulty Trail. Trees along the Upper Faulty Trail are marked with square blazes cut into their trunks, unique to the Sandias.

Extending your hike: Because Faulty Trail crosses several other trails there are many possibilities for making loop hikes. One of my favorites is to start from the Canyon Estates trailhead and hike up the Crest Trail to Upper Faulty Trail. Take Upper Faulty to its junction with Lower Faulty, then hike south to the Crest Trail, and back to the starting point. This makes a nice 5.5 mile circuit through the southern end of the Sandias.

Oso Corredor Trail (No. 265)

Length: 2.7 miles (one way)
Elevation: 7,810–8,600 feet
Rating: Easy
See Map: 2 (page 35)
Driving Instructions: Oso Corredor Trail is usually accessed via Bill Spring Trail or Tree Spring Trail. To start from Bill Spring Trail, take I-40 east from Albuquerque, go north on NM 14 for about six miles, and turn west

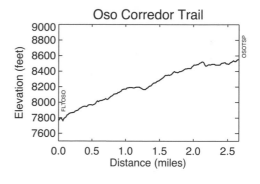

onto the Crest Highway, NM 536. Drive two miles and then turn into the Doc Long Picnic area. The parking area for Bill Spring Trail is to the right (wp BSPTH). To start from Tree Spring Trail, from the junction with NM 14 drive 5.6 miles up the Crest Highway to the Tree Spring trailhead (wp TSPTH), on the left side of the road.

Description

Oso Corredor is a beautiful trail on the east side of the Sandias. The tree cover makes for a cool outing in the summer. A surprising amount of snow cover usually remains through May along the upper portion of the trail, which can almost make it impassable before the warm weather sets in.

The trail was completed in the 1989. Its name, Spanish for "running bear," commemorates an extremely dry summer and fall that year, which saw a record number of bears venturing into the foothills in search of food.

Fig. 6. Oso Corredor Trail in early spring.

Oso Corredor lies interior to the Sandia trail system, so you must hike other trails to reach it. The entire length of the trail falls outside the Sandia Mountain Wilderness, and mountain bikers also use this route. If you are on foot, yield the right-of-way to a bike rider.

The easiest access to the southeast starting point of Oso Corredor Trail is via Bill Spring Trail. Drive or walk to the far end of the Doc Long Picnic Ground to find the trailhead for Bill Spring Trail (wp BSPTH), and hike its 0.7 mile length. Then go south 0.25 mile on Faulty Trail to the junction with Oso Corredor Trail (wp FLTOSO).

From that point Oso Corredor Trail gains about four hundred feet in elevation in the first half mile. After reaching the top of a ridge the trail gently contours to the northwest for the next couple of miles. In this pleasant area, the heavy ponderosa pine cover prevents scenic views along the way. Wildflowers abound along the trail in spring and early summer. You may see earthstar mushrooms (cute, but inedible) growing near the trail. About two miles along Oso Corredor Trail, the trail reaches a significant rise, a couple of hundred feet above a hairpin curve in the Crest Highway. The final portion of Oso Corredor Trail parallels the road on a

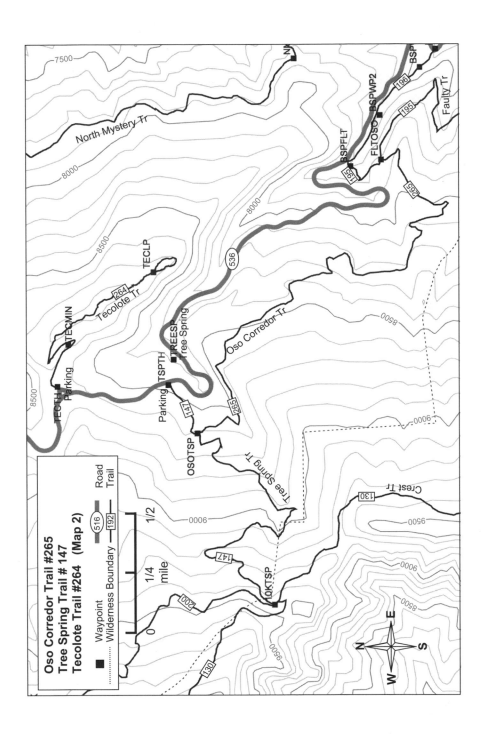

Oso Corredor Trail #265
Tree Spring Trail # 147
Tecolote Trail #264 (Map 2)

Waypoint
Wilderness Boundary

516 Road
192 Trail

0   1/4   1/2
        mile

north-facing slope. This section of the trail can remain snow packed and icy until late spring (until May in some years). The footing can be treacherous, so please be careful.

After turning north from the slope, Oso Corredor Trail enters a final stretch of grassy meadow. In the summer the area is beautiful with grasses and wildflowers. A couple of wooden footbridges cross small streambeds through this section. Shortly afterward, Oso Corredor meets Tree Spring Trail (wp OSOTSP) about 0.3 mile west of the Tree Spring trailhead (wp TSPTH).

Tree Spring Trail (No. 147)

Length: 2 miles (one way)
Elevation: 8,470–9,440 feet
Rating: Moderate
See Map: 2 (page 35)
Driving Instructions: Take I-40 east from Albuquerque, go north on NM 14 for about six miles, and take the turnoff to the Crest Highway, NM 536. Drive 5.6 miles to the Tree Spring parking area on the left side of the road (wp TSPTH).

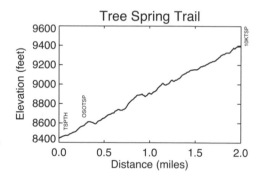

Description

Tree Spring Trail is one of the most popular trails in the Sandia Mountains. With a modest elevation gain of 880 feet over its two-mile length, it is an enjoyable hike to the main Sandia ridgeline. On a typical weekend the parking area is full. For that reason, I like to visit this trail on weekdays, when the area is more peaceful.

The trail's name comes from a spring that was found flowing from beneath a large tree stump below the current trailhead. This spring is just north of NM 536 about a half mile before you reach the Tree Spring Trail parking area (wp TREESP). It is concealed by dense foliage and barely

Fig. 7. Information sign near Tree Spring trailhead.

visible from the road. There remains some old stonework around the spring, probably built by the CCC in the 1930s.

Tree Spring Trail passes the junction with Oso Corredor Trail (wp OSOTSP) about a third of a mile from the parking area. The climb toward the ridge is lined with thick firs, ascending into aspen and scrub oak. Keep an eye out for wildflowers in the meadows along the way during the spring and summer months aside this wide and well-worn trail.

At about two miles, you reach the Sandia Mountain Wilderness boundary, marked by a wooden fence at the end of Tree Spring Trail (wp 10KTSP). This spot forms a significant juncture of trails leading in four directions. A wooden sign points to the south for the hike to Canyon Estates via the Crest Trail (13 miles), uphill to the Upper Tram Terminal (Summit House) (1.5 miles), north to 10K Trail (which has its southern termination at this point), and downhill to Tree Spring Trail.

There is a beautiful overlook near the Crest Trail just above this four-trail junction via a 200' path to the west. It is a must-see location, and is a great spot for a snack and enjoying the views of Albuquerque and the Rio Grande Valley.

Extending your hike: I recommend continuing your hike to the Summit House (Upper Tram Terminal). There are beautiful vistas to the west across precipitous cliffs from the ridgeline. The hike from Tree Spring Trail to the Tram has a significant uphill grade in places. Reward yourself with lunch at the Tram Terminal restaurant, or on the patio at the outdoor grill, which operates on summer weekends.

Tecolote Trail (No. 264)

Length: 1.3 miles (one way)
Elevation: 8,630–8,810 feet
Rating: Easy
See Map: 2 (page 35)
Driving Instructions: Drive east from Albuquerque on I-40, north on NM 14 for six miles, and take the Crest Highway (NM 536) up the mountain. The turnoff for Tecolote Trail is just a few yards past the green six-mile marker on NM 536, at the exit for Dry Camp Picnic Ground (wp TECTH).

Description

Tecolote Trail is one of the newer additions to the Sandia Mountain trail system. Tecolote (Spanish for "owl") Trail travels to Tecolote Peak, where you will be rewarded with 360° views. This trail may be snow covered in the winter.

Tecolote Trail initially has several broad switchbacks to make the modest gain in elevation up a slope to reach the ridge top. After only a few minutes on Tecolote Trail, you will pass a mine shaft, just to your left (wp TECMIN). The first portion of the trail is densely tree covered and verdant.

Once gaining the ridge top, the Tecolote Trail continues in a southeasterly direction. Along the way, notice the views of the Crest Highway below and the Sandia Peak Ski Area to the west. About one mile into the hike, you will come to a brown signpost (wp TECLP) marking the start of a quarter-mile end loop that forms the turnaround portion of this trail.

Balsam Glade Nature Trail

Length: 0.3 mile (one way)
Elevation: 8,620–8,660 feet
Rating: Easy
See Map: 3 (page 40)
Driving Instructions: To find Balsam Glade Picnic Area, drive east from Albuquerque on I-40 to the Tijeras exit, then north on NM 14 about six miles to the Crest Highway (NM 536). Balsam Glade Picnic Area is 7.3 miles up the Crest Highway, with a parking area on the right (north) side of the road (wp BALTH). The parking area is also the turnoff to NM 165W, which goes to Placitas through Las Huertas Canyon.

Description

The well-maintained Balsam Glade Nature Trail begins at the Balsam Glade Picnic Area. It is well suited for hikers from ages two to ninety. The short nature trail leads to an overlook above Madera Canyon. The nature trail would be a good place to take an out-of-town visitor who might not be able to manage a more demanding mountain hike.

The area is misnamed for Balsam Fir, which is a tree species found in the northeastern United States. The white fir growing in the area appears similar to the balsam fir. Early settlers misnamed the tree, and the original name stuck over the years. Other trees in the area include ponderosa pine and Gambel oak, with raspberry and snowberry bushes growing along the path.

The trail, about 0.3 mile in length, has little elevation gain. There are benches and informative signs along the route discussing the wildlife and ecosystem of the area. On the short walk, you pass the ruins of a YMCA camp dating back to the 1930s. An overlook at the end of the trail (wp BALOBS) provides handsome views across Madera Canyon to the south, as well as the eastern slopes of the Sandia Mountains.

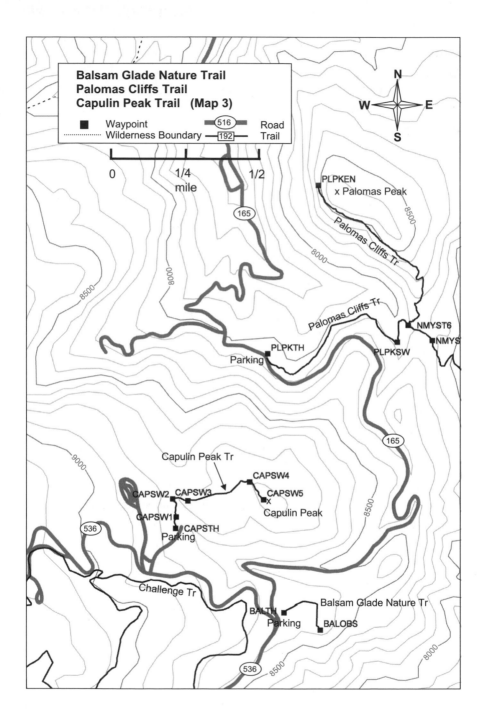

Balsam Glade Nature Trail
Palomas Cliffs Trail
Capulin Peak Trail (Map 3)

■ Waypoint   516   Road
········· Wilderness Boundary   192   Trail

0   1/4   1/2
       mile

N
W   E
S

PLPKEN
x Palomas Peak

Palomas Cliffs Tr

8500

8000

8000

8500

165

Palomas Cliffs Tr

NMYST6
NMYS

PLPKTH
Parking

PLPKSW

165

9000

Capulin Peak Tr

CAPSW4
CAPSW2 CAPSW3
CAPSW5
x
Capulin Peak

CAPSW1
CAPSTH
Parking

8500

536

Challenge Tr

Balsam Glade Nature Tr

BALTH
Parking
BALOBS

8000

536

8500

10K Trail (No. 200)

Length: 4.7 miles (one way)
Elevation: 9,440–10,040 feet
Rating: Moderate
See Map: 4 (page 42)
Driving Instructions: To find the 10K trailhead, drive east from Albuquerque on I-40, north on NM 14 for six miles, and up the Crest Highway (NM 536) eleven miles to the 10K Trail parking lot on the right (north) side of the road

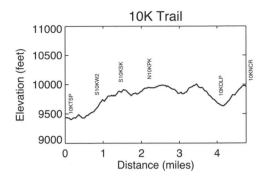

(wp N10KPK). A smaller parking lot is available on the south side of the road (wp S10KPK) for convenient access to the southern portion of 10K Trail.

Description

The 10K Trail runs from the upper end of Tree Spring Trail (at the Crest Trail junction) to Del Agua Overlook. It roughly follows the ten-thousand-foot elevation contour, from which the trail gets its name ("K" being shorthand for "kilo," or one thousand). This cool, tree-covered trail provides an ideal hike from late spring to fall. Because of its elevation, 10K Trail is usually snow covered in winter, and is used as a cross country ski trail. Most of 10K Trail lies outside the Sandia Mountain Wilderness boundary. Mountain bikes are allowed except for the portion from Ellis Trail to Del Agua Overlook.

Because of its location near the main ridgeline and the Crest Highway, 10K Trail can be combined with other popular trails in the area to form loop hikes. For example, hike north on 10K Trail from the parking area to Del Agua Overlook, then south on the Crest Trail (to a second waiting car). A similar hike goes south on 10K Trail from the Crest Highway to the Crest Trail, and then north along the Crest Trail, past the Upper Tram Terminal to the Crest parking lot.

From the south, 10K Trail begins at the junction of the Tree Spring Trail and the Crest Trail (wp 10KTSP). The 10K Trail travels north through thick scrub oak, with occasional openings and good views to the east. After about one half mile, the trail gets steeper as it rises out of Madera Canyon toward

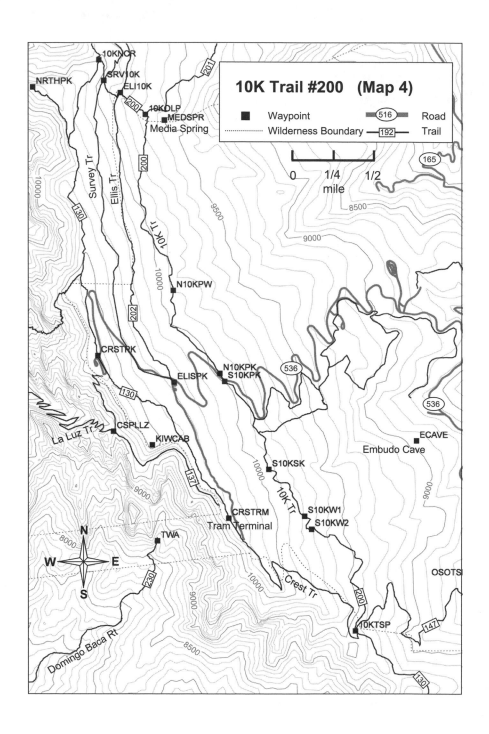

the southern edge of the Sandia Peak Ski runs (wp S10KW2). Be careful when hiking across the ski runs to make sure that you see where 10K Trail reenters the woods on the opposite side. It is easy to lose sight of the trail as you cross the grassy ski runs in the summer. Each time you reach the edge of a ski run, look for a blue diamond marker on a tree at the opposite side as you cross over. From the northernmost ski run (wp S10KSK), it is about another half mile hike north to the parking area and Crest Highway.

The trail continues from the north side of the road and a larger parking area (wp N10KPK). After 1.75 miles 10K Trail reaches the southern trailhead of Osha Loop Trail (wp 10KOLP). A spur trail leads down to Media Spring, which is 0.15 mile from this junction (wp MEDSPR). 10K Trail heads west and begins a steady climb toward the ridgeline. The trail soon crosses Ellis Trail (wp ELI10K) and then Survey Trail (wp SRV10K). Shortly afterward, 10K Trail intersects the Crest Trail (wp 10KNCR) overlooking Del Agua Canyon.

Each year between mid-September and early October, I usually hike the north portion of 10K Trail to see the spectacular golden aspen leaves along the trail and at Del Agua Overlook. Be sure to take a camera. I can almost guarantee that you will find other visitors there to take your picture in front of the fall colors.

Extending your hike: You can take a pleasant three-mile extension on north 10K Trail by hiking Osha Loop Trail beginning either at its southern trailhead (1.75 miles north of the Crest Highway) or the northwest trailhead (about a half mile north of Del Agua Overlook on the Crest Trail).

Ellis Trail (No. 202)

Length: 3.2 miles (one way)
Elevation: 9,640–10,270 feet
Rating: Moderate
See Map: 5 (page 46)
Driving Instructions: To reach the trailhead for this hike, head east from Albuquerque on I-40, north on NM 14 for 6 miles, and up the Crest Highway (NM 536) 12.1 miles to the Ellis Trail parking lot on the left (south) side of the road (wp ELISPK).

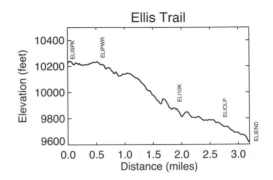

Description

Ellis Trail follows a wide road cut that was denuded of trees in the late 1960s in an ill-conceived plan to construct a highway from Sandia Crest to Placitas. The project was eventually stopped, and the road cut has become a manmade meadow. These days, Ellis Trail probably gets more usage from cross-country skiers than from hikers. It offers good views to the north and east along its 3.2-mile length.

Ellis Trail is named after George Ellis, who lived in the Sandia Mountains from the 1880s until his death in 1912. Ellis Ranch is about 2.5 miles north of the Balsam Glade turnoff on NM 165W, in Las Huertas Canyon.

Hiking north on Ellis Trail from the parking area, you walk along an old jeep road. After two-thirds of a mile, the trail encounters a large embankment (perhaps thirty feet high). The jeep trail curves off to the east, but Ellis Trail continues north and over this obstacle. The easy going trail continues up and down small ravines along the way. About two miles into the hike, Ellis Trail crosses 10K Trail (wp ELI10K). (The Del Agua Overlook, wp 10KNCR, is a short hike west on 10K Trail from here.) Continuing north on Ellis Trail, you cross Osha Loop Trail (wp ELIOLP) after about another two-thirds of a mile.

Ellis Trail fades to obscurity about a third of a mile north of the intersection with Osha Loop Trail (wp ELIEND). From the north end of Ellis Trail, you can bushwhack through the scrub oak trees another fifty yards to the north and end up on the Crest Trail at the North Del Agua Overlook.

Fig. 8. Aspens lining Ellis Trail in the fall.

Extending your hike: To vary the scenery on the way back, from the north end of Ellis Trail bushwhack north to the Crest Trail (as mentioned above) and hike south for about one mile to the junction with 10 K Trail at Del Agua Overlook (wp 10KNCR). Go southeast on 10K Trail about a quarter of a mile to Ellis Trail (wp ELI10K) and take Ellis Trail south to your car.

For a more significant extension, hike south on either Ellis Trail or the Crest Trail to pick up the northern portion of Osha Loop trail (at either wp ELIOLP or wp NCROLP) and follow Osha Loop about two miles in a clockwise direction to the junction with 10K Trail. Continue to the northwest (not the south branch) on 10K Trail for 0.25 mile to pick-up Ellis Trail (wp ELI10K), then return south on Ellis Trail to your car.

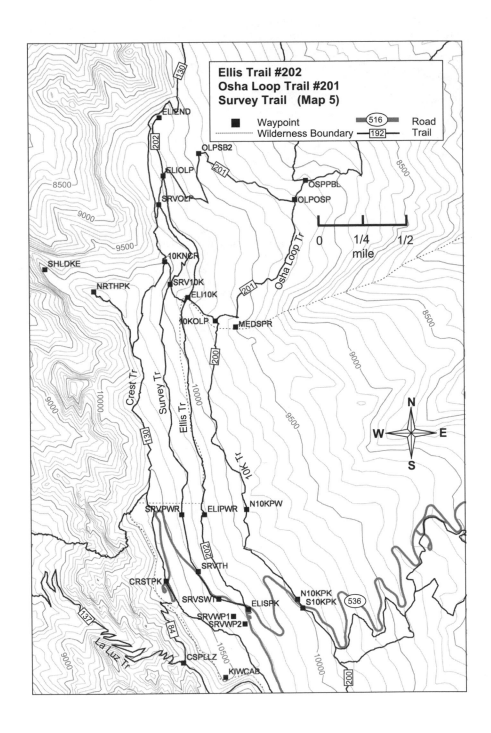

Ellis Trail #202
Osha Loop Trail #201
Survey Trail   (Map 5)

Waypoint ■
Wilderness Boundary ·······
516 Road
192 Trail

0   1/4   1/2
mile

N
W   E
S

ELI2ND
OLPSB2
ELIOLP
SRVOLP
201
OSPPBL
OLPOSP
Osha Loop Tr
SHLDKE
10KNCR
SRV10K
ELI10K
NRTHPK
10KOLP
MEDSPR
201
200
Crest Tr
Survey Tr
Ellis Tr
130
10K Tr
SRVPWR
ELIPWR
N10KPW
202
SRVTH
CRSTPK
SRVSW1
ELISPK
N10KPK
S10KPK
536
SRVWP1
SRVWP2
84
137
La Luz Tr
CSPLLZ
KIWCAB
200

Osha Loop Trail (No. 201)

Length: 2.4 miles (one way)
Elevation: 9,210–9,740 feet
Rating: Moderate
See Map: 5 (page 46)
Driving Instructions: Osha Loop Trail begins 1.75 miles north of the Crest Highway, and must be reached by hiking other trails. The most convenient access to Osha Loop Trail is by the Crest Trail or 10 K Trail. For the 10K trailhead, drive east

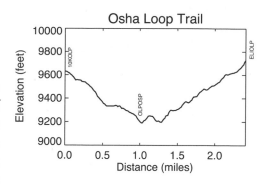

from Albuquerque on I-40, north on NM 14 for six miles, and up the Crest Highway (NM 536) eleven miles to the 10K Trail parking lot on the right (north) side of the road (wp N10KPK).

Description

Osha Loop Trail adds a beautiful, well-shaded interior trail to the Sandia Mountain trail system. You have to hike some distance along other trails to reach it. Osha Loop Trail itself forms about two-thirds of a closed loop, and it can combine with short portions of the Crest Trail and 10K Trail to make a 3.5 mile loop.

The name of the trail comes from the medicinal plant "osha" (*Ligusticum porteri*) found in the area. The osha plant inhabits dry meadows in the West. When in bloom, osha has a beautiful white flower. The plant finds modern use as a decongestant and as a tonic for the respiratory and upper digestive systems.

Hike north on 10K Trail for 1.75 miles to reach the southern end of Osha Loop Trail (wp 10KOLP). Osha Loop heads to the northeast, passing a scenic overlook above Media Canyon after 0.15 miles. The trail steadily drops about four hundred feet in elevation over the next mile, and reaches the junction with Osha Spring Trail (wp OLPOSP), an old mining road that heads down into Las Huertas Canyon.

From the junction with Osha Spring Trail, Osha Loop heads northwest toward the main Sandia ridgeline, climbing about five hundred vertical feet in a mile and a half. Along the way, Osha Loop Trail intersects Ellis

Trail at a broad clearing (wp ELIOLP) and the northern terminus of Survey Trail (wp SRVOLP). Osha Loop Trail ends at its junction with the Crest Trail (wp OLPNCR), overlooking Del Agua Canyon. To close the loop, hike south on the Crest Trail for 0.3 mile to Del Agua Overlook (wp 10KNCR), then southeast on 10K Trail one half mile to the southern starting point of Osha Loop (wp 10KOLP).

Extending your hike: Because Osha Loop Trail intersects several other trails in the area, there are any number of side trips that you can take. From the intersection of 10K Trail and Osha Loop Trail (wp 10KOLP), a short (0.15 mile) but steep side trail goes east to Media Spring (wp MEDSPR) in a lush meadow. The trail to Media Spring branches to the east from Osha Loop Trail about twenty yards north of its junction with 10K Trail.

From the northeast portion of Osha Loop Trail, at the junction with Osha Spring Trail (wp OLPOSP), you have the option of hiking north to Peñasco Blanco Trail and the nearby Osha Spring. From the northwest portion of Osha Loop Trail, you may also head north or south on either the Crest Trail or Ellis Trail, or south on Survey Trail. These areas are shaded and cool in the summer and make for more beautiful hiking.

Chimney Canyon Route (No. 137A)

Length: 1.7 miles (one way)
Elevation: 8,150–10,590 feet
Rating: Most Difficult
See Map: 6 (page 52)
Driving Instructions: Go east on I-40 from Albuquerque, north on NM 14 for 6 miles, drive up the Crest Highway (NM 536) for 13.4 miles to the top of the mountain, and park at the main parking lot (wp CRSTPK).

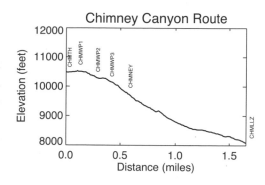

Warning: This is one of the most potentially dangerous hikes in the Sandia Mountains. The first hour goes almost straight down the mountain in a very remote area. The Chimney Canyon Route is not an officially maintained trail. Don't attempt this hike unless you are well prepared physically and able to take care of yourself in the event of a mishap in the wilderness. If you complete the hike as described, you will be challenged with four hours or more of very strenuous hiking.

Description

Chimney Canyon Route is an adventure that I enjoy, but it is not for the casual hiker. The route follows Chimney Canyon from below the radio towers atop Sandia Crest to meet La Luz Trail about halfway down the mountain. The route that I suggest is to hike down the trail rather than up; this I recommend for several reasons. First, if you were to hike it from the bottom, you would have at least a two-hour hike down the Crest Spur Trail and La Luz Trail to even reach the lower trailhead. That hike will tax the energy you need for the hardest part of the hike, that is, Chimney Canyon Route itself. The trail is incredibly steep. Having hiked the route in both directions, I think it is much easier to climb down the steep slope than to go up it. (However, care is required in either direction.) The trail is also somewhat hard to follow. I know that it is easier to see the trail in front of you when you are looking from above than from below. When I have hiked up the trail it has been very difficult for me to follow. (You don't want to get lost on this hike.) Finally, the trail is difficult to find from the lower trailhead; I can tell you exactly how to get there from the top.

Of course, the problem is that once you've hiked down Chimney Canyon Route, you are a two-hour hike away from your transportation home. That is a problem. You have two choices. I usually take the hike up La Luz Trail, and then take the Crest Spur Trail over to my car. That makes for a difficult but beautiful day's hike. Another alternative is to leave a second car in the La Luz parking area, and hike down La Luz Trail. This involves some logistics and extra driving time, which is why I prefer the first choice.

Start the hike by walking north along the Crest Trail from the parking lot. (There are several forks and branches in the route described in this paragraph, below. Pay close attention, or it is unlikely that you will find Chimney Canyon Route. Once you're past this section, the directions themselves are easy.) After a half mile on the Crest Trail, you will reach a small sign (wp CHMTH) that says Del Agua Overlook 1.5 Mi. This sign marks the best access to the Chimney Canyon Route. (In the "old days" one could just walk through the area of the radio towers, and drop down to the Chimney Canyon Route. That area is now restricted to the public.) Just to the left of this sign is a trail heading west. This little trail immediately forks, and you want to follow the left branch around to the south. After a few hundred yards, you will reach another fork in this trail (wp CHMWP1). One branch goes east (left), and upward to the radio towers (the old access point). You want to take the **right** fork to continue down the mountain. However, you will immediately encounter another branch in the trail after only twenty feet. From here, the left branch heads over to Crest Spur trail (I took this path once by mistake). Chimney Canyon Route is the **right**, downhill branch. The trail is easy to follow after getting past these few branch points. If you think you're not on the right path and have a GPS, use it to navigate to the waypoint CHMWP2.

The trail begins to take a more southerly tack after this section. About a half mile from the "Del Agua" sign, you will reach a distinct aspen grove (wp CHMWP2) on a saddle point. The grass is thick, and it can be hard to follow the trail through this grove. The proper route is to continue south through the grassy area. The trail then drops downhill through more aspens.

The downward slope begins to get steep; soon it becomes incredibly steep. The trail descends a significant rock slide (*couloir*), which takes a lot of patience and scrambling to get down (wp CHMWP3). At least I'd have to say that the route is well worn and easy to see (if not easy to scramble down) the whole way. Be mindful of safety as you go down this steep chute. Rocks can easily become dislodged and tumble down on a hiking partner below you. For this reason, it is a good idea to stay close together as you go down; in case a rock starts rolling down the slope it won't have time to pick up much momentum when it reaches your partner if you are near one another. Also, be very careful of your balance and footing along the way.

You will eventually make your way down to the base of the Chimney (wp CHMNEY), a 150-foot-tall rock formation from which the canyon gets its name. The rest of the way down Chimney Canyon Route is relatively easy hiking, although the path is indistinct in many places. After a while, the trail takes a significant jog to the north keeping well above the canyon bottom. The trail stays along the northern slope of the canyon as the ground turns to sandy soil. You reach the intersection with La Luz Trail (wp CHMLLZ) after about a mile hike from the Chimney. Sometimes there is a small cairn (pile of rocks) on the opposite side of La Luz Trail, marking the point where you have just come out. This spot is about one hundred yards downhill from the point that La Luz Trail crosses the stream that runs down from Chimney Canyon.

From this location, you may either walk down La Luz Trail (where you'd better have another car waiting), or up La Luz Trail. If you choose to hike back to the Crest, follow La Luz Trail to the junction with the Crest Spur Trail (wp CSPLLZ). Take the left fork (toward the north) continuing up the Crest Spur Trail to the parking area (wp CRSTPK), ending a rugged and memorable hiking day.

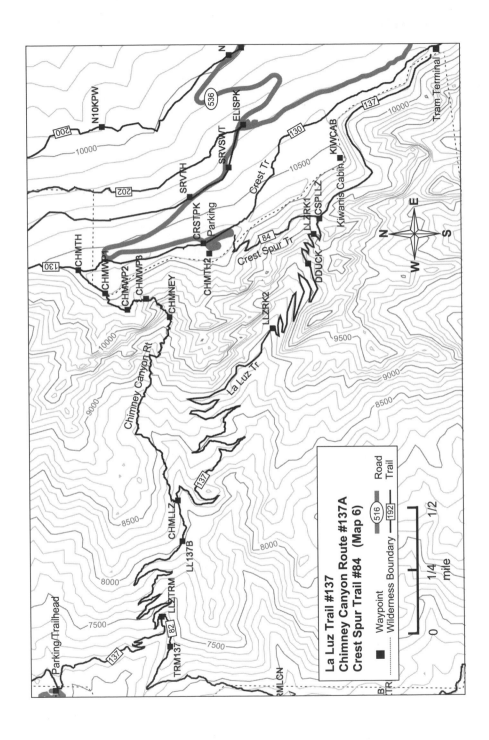

La Luz Trail #137
Chimney Canyon Route #137A
Crest Spur Trail #84 (Map 6)

■ Waypoint
⋯⋯ Wilderness Boundary

Road
Trail

516 Road
192 Trail

0   1/4   1/2
mile

Length: 0.6 mile (one way)
Elevation: 10,100–10,610 feet
Rating: Easy
See Map: 6 (page 52)
Driving Instructions: Take I-40 east from Albuquerque, go north on NM 14 for 6 miles, drive up the Crest Highway (NM 536) for 13.4 miles to the top of the mountain, and park at the main parking lot (wp CRSTPK).

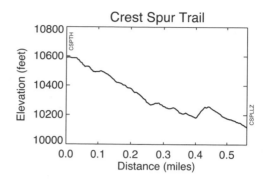

Description

Crest Spur Trail is a short trail that receives a lot of traffic because of its close proximity to Sandia Crest. Hundreds of thousands of people drive the Sandia Crest National Scenic Byway (NM 536) to visit the Crest each year. The Crest Spur Trail begins at the south end of the Crest House (wp CSPTH), marked by signs. This trail provides access to La Luz Trail, and also enables a nice loop hike for walking south to the Upper Tram Terminal (Summit House) when combined with La Luz Trail and the Crest Trail (No. 130).

The Crest Spur Trail quickly drops below the main ridgeline from the trailhead. Four hundred feet from the trailhead the trail makes a switchback to the south (wp CSPSW1). From this point a faint, crude trail leads north providing an alternate access to Chimney Canyon Route, meeting it just below the radio towers (wp CHMWP1). The well-worn Crest Spur Trail continues to the south with a signpost and arrow pointing the way.

After passing through a stand of quaking aspens the Crest Spur Trail passes the boundary to the Sandia Mountain Wilderness. The trail goes down a steep stone staircase 0.35 miles from the trailhead (wp CSPWP1). Horseback travel on the Crest Spur Trail is prohibited specifically because of this obstacle. From this point the trail continues southward along a considerably less steep grade. The Crest Spur Trail ends at its junction with La Luz Trail (wp CSPLLZ).

Extending your hike: From its junction with the Crest Spur Trail, La Luz Trail travels south about one mile to the Upper Tram Terminal, Visitor's Center, and the High Finance Restaurant (wp CRSTRM). To make a pleasant loop hike, you can hike back to your car by taking the Crest Trail (No. 130) north. This route takes you past Kiwanis Meadow and the beautiful overlook at Kiwanis Cabin.

La Luz Trail also heads down the mountain approximately seven miles from the junction with the Crest Spur Trail to the Juan Tabo trailhead. Many people hiking up La Luz Trail take the Crest Spur Trail in order to hike to Sandia Crest, rather than continuing south to the Upper Tram Terminal.

Crest Nature Trail (No. 98)

Length: 0.2 miles (round trip)
Elevation: 10,600 feet
Rating: Easy
See Map: not included
Driving Instructions: Take I-40 east from Albuquerque, go north on NM 14 for 6 miles, drive up the Crest Highway (NM 536) for 13.4 miles to the top of the mountain, and park at the main parking lot (wp CRSTPK).

Description
The Crest Nature Trail provides a nice introduction to the plant life and ecosystem of the Sandia Mountains. The trail can be followed on a self-guided tour, using the many informative signs. Forest Service rangers also offer guided tours along the nature trail a number of times every day. Children can earn a Junior Ranger badge or patch by picking up a questionnaire, walking the nature trail, and answering the questions by reading the signs along the way. Inquire at the desk inside the Crest House for more information.

The Crest Nature Trail begins south of the Crest House at the far end of the lower parking lot. Follow a cement path south past the restroom facilities for a hundred yards, or so. At the end of the pavement is a "Welcome" sign (wp CRSTNT), marking the beginning of the short loop trail. The east branch of the trail travels roughly along the ridgeline, and features many signs identifying the common trees of the mountain. At the far end of the loop, the trail opens up to beautiful views to the south and west; you also have a nice view of La Luz Trail several hundred feet below as it switchbacks across the talus slope of upper La Cueva Canyon. From the overlook, the trail descends some tight limestone steps beginning the trip north to complete the short loop.

Extending your hike: From the sign at the south end of the Crest Nature Trail you can pick up the Crest Trail (No. 130) and hike south about 0.5 mile to Kiwanis Cabin (wp KIWCAB), or hike about 1.5 miles to the Upper Tram Terminal (wp CRSTRM).

Peak Nature Trail (No. 97)

Length: 0.3 miles (round trip)
Elevation: 10,300 feet
Rating: Easy
See Map: not included
Driving Instructions: The Peak Nature Trail is just north of the Sandia Peak Aerial Tramway upper terminal. The heaviest use of the nature trail is by people who have ridden the Tram to the top of the mountain. Alternately, drive east from Albuquerque on I-40, go north on NM 14 for 6 miles, drive up the Crest Highway (NM 536) for 13.4 miles to the top of the mountain, and park at the main parking lot (wp CRSTPK). Hike 1.5 miles south on the Crest Trail (No. 130) to reach the Peak Nature Trail.

Description

This short nature trail gives visitors an overview of the Sandia Mountain ecosystem. The trail can be taken as a self-guided tour, following the many signs along the way. The Forest Service also offers guided tours throughout the day; inquire at the information desk inside the Upper Tram Terminal. Children can earn a Junior Ranger badge or patch by picking up a questionnaire, walking the nature trail, and answering the questions by reading the signs along the way. Inquire about details at the Forest Service information desk in the Upper Tram Terminal.

To find the trail, walk north from the High Finance Restaurant to the end of the asphalt (wp CRSTRM). From this point, La Luz Trail branches to the west, the Crest Trail heads north, and to the east is a sign marking the trailhead for the Peak Nature Trail. Along the nature trail you will learn how to identify many of the trees common to the area, how to tell the difference between a fir and a spruce (do you know?) and perhaps see some mountain wildflowers. At the northern end, the nature trail goes down some steps protected by a metal railing. As the trail makes its way back south, you will be treated to a beautiful overlook across Domingo Baca Canyon to the west. The Peak Nature Trail terminates when it joins the Crest Trail (No. 130) about one hundred yards north of the starting point.

Extending your hike: Kiwanis Cabin is a popular destination for visitors to the top of the Tram. Hike north on the Crest Trail about one mile, following the signs to Kiwanis Cabin (wp KIWCAB).

Peñasco Blanco Trail (No. 334)

Length: 1.6 miles (one way)

Special Note: A round-trip hike of at least eight miles is required (see below)

Elevation: 8,450–9,110 feet

Rating: Moderate

See Map: 7 (page 59)

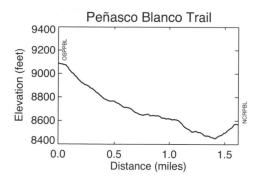

Driving Instructions: Drive east from Albuquerque on I-40 to the Tijeras exit, then north on NM 14 about six miles to the Crest Highway (NM 536). Take the Crest Highway all the way to the top of the mountain (13.4 miles), and park in the main parking lot (wp CRSTPK).

Description

Peñasco Blanco Trail is a "connector trail" within the Sandia Mountains, meaning that there isn't a trailhead at a parking area, so you must hike other trails to reach it. It is a several-mile hike from any direction to reach Peñasco Blanco Trail. The route described here is a good way to hike Peñasco Blanco, as well as to see much of the northern portion of the Crest Trail. Be warned that although Peñasco Blanco Trail is only 1.6 miles long, the hike described below totals 9 miles in length.

I suggest hiking north along the Crest Trail from the Crest parking area (wp CRSTPK) for 4.5 miles to reach Peñasco Blanco's northern trailhead (wp NCRPBL), then hiking south on Peñasco Blanco Trail toward your car, forming a loop. Another access to Peñasco Blanco's north end is to hike south for 5.5 miles on the Crest Trail from the Tunnel Spring trailhead. Peñasco Blanco Trail can also be reached by hiking north for 1.5 miles on 10K Trail, then another mile north on Osha Loop and Osha Spring Trails to reach the south trailhead (wp OSPPBL).

To reach the northern trailhead, as I have suggested, begin by hiking north along the Crest Trail from the Crest parking area. Along the 4.5 mile hike to reach Peñasco Blanco Trail you will pass the beautiful Del Agua Overlook (wp 10KNCR), and junctions with 10K Trail and Osha Loop Trail. Along this route the Crest Trail drops about twenty-two

Fig. 9. Peñasco Blanco rock formation.

hundred feet in elevation by the time you reach the Peñasco Blanco trailhead (wp NCRPBL).

A large gray wall of limestone can be seen (in profile) to the east from the Crest Trail as you approach the trailhead. This formation is Peñasco Blanco, Spanish for "white bluff," from which the trail takes its name. The rock formation is also sometimes called the China Wall.

The trail was built in 1982 by a group called the Sandia Mountain Wildlife and Conservation Association. Rick Davis of the group discovered an obscure and overgrown trail leading north from the Osha Spring meadow. In clearing the trail the group followed the original route as closely as possible, using blaze marks that were still visible on the ponderosa pines. The route was originally used by homesteaders for access to Osha Spring, and continued toward Placitas, past the current northern trailhead at the Crest Trail (wp NCRPBL). The group originally called the route the China Wall Trail.

Peñasco Blanco Trail goes south from the Crest Trail junction through thickets of Gambel oak. The trail maintains a modest elevation grade, gaining only 650 feet in elevation over its 1.6-mile length. It often cuts a

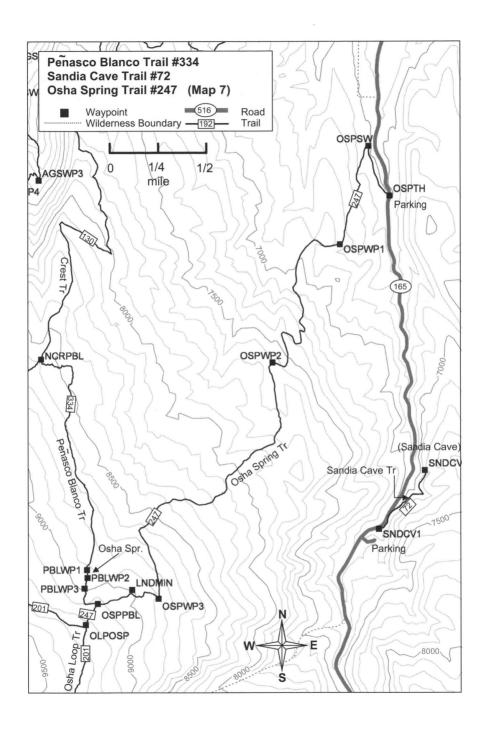

Peñasco Blanco Trail #334
Sandia Cave Trail #72
Osha Spring Trail #247 (Map 7)

■ Waypoint
·············· Wilderness Boundary
⬭516⬭ Road
▱192▱ Trail

0   1/4   1/2
     mile

OSPSW
OSPTH
Parking
247
OSPWP1
165
AGSWP3
P4
130
Crest Tr
7000
7500
8000
NCRPBL
OSPWP2
334
Peñasco Blanco Tr
7000
8500
Osha Spring Tr
(Sandia Cave)
Sandia Cave Tr
SNDCV
247
72
7500
SNDCV1
Parking
9000
Osha Spr.
PBLWP1
PBLWP2
LNDMIN
PBLWP3
OSPWP3
201
247
OSPPBL
Osha Loop Tr
OLPOSP
201
9500
9000
8500
8000
8000
N
W   E
S

narrow path through the trees, but occasionally opens up for views to the south and east.

About 1.25 miles along Peñasco Blanco Trail, the route nears Osha Spring. This area is wide open, with hardly any trees. There are large sections of soft, gray soil, produced by precipitated calcite from abundant lime in the groundwater. Peñasco Blanco Trail is difficult to discern along this stretch, although a couple of vertical trail-marker posts and cairns mark the way. Osha Spring is just to the east of the trail in a brush thicket. There is usually a pool of water fed by a pipe from the spring.

Make your way the couple of hundred yards across the meadow, heading toward the tree line and a bearing slightly west of south. Just at the tree line the ground turns firmer and the trail is again visible (wp PBLWP3). Once on the well-worn trail through the wooded area, you will reach the intersection with Osha Spring Trail (wp OSPPBL) a few hundred yards later, marked by a trail sign. This is the southern trailhead of Peñasco Blanco Trail.

From here, you are still about three miles from your car, so I recommend taking the shortest route home. Hike south on Osha Spring Trail for a couple of hundred yards (wp OLPOSP), then take the left (southern) branch of Osha Loop Trail. After about a mile on Osha Loop Trail, you will reach 10K Trail (wp 10KOLP), marked by a signpost. From here, follow 10K Trail to the right (northwest) on a steady uphill climb (crossing Ellis Trail) to its intersection with the Crest Trail (wp 10KNCR). From this spot it is a 1.8-mile walk (still uphill) to the Crest parking area (wp CRSTPK).

Length: 0.5 mile (one way)
Elevation: 7,040–7,180 feet
Rating: Easy
See Map: 7 (page 59)
Driving Instructions: Take I-25 north from Albuquerque, then exit 242 east to Placitas. Drive east through Placitas, and continue as the road turns south for about a three-mile drive along the rough dirt road. You will see the parking lot (wp SNDCV1) after the fifth one-lane bridge. A sign on the east side of the road marks the turnoff.

Description

Sandia Cave is one of the most important archaeological sites of prehistoric man on the American continent. It was discovered in 1927, and excavation was begun in 1936. Artifacts up to two thousand years old were found in the upper layers of the cave's recesses. Breaking through a limestone crust, archaeologists discovered stone tools from the Folsom culture, dating back six thousand to ten thousand years. The cave is registered as a National Historic Landmark.

The cave itself is high in the eastern wall of Las Huertas Canyon. It extends more than 450 feet into the mountain with a downward slope of nine degrees. Sandia Cave is seven to ten feet in diameter for its entire length.

It is a short half-mile walk to Sandia Cave, just slightly uphill. Climb the spiral staircase to the cave itself at the end of the trail (wp SNDCV2). There are beautiful views of the eastern slopes of the mountain from a small observation deck. Exploration past the cave's opening is discouraged. The cliffs in the vicinity of the cave are a popular rock-climbing location for experienced climbers.

Osha Spring Trail (No. 247)

Length: 4.3 miles (one way)
Elevation: 6,500–9,110 feet
Rating: Difficult
See Map: 7 (page 59)
Driving Instructions: To find Osha Spring Trail, drive north on I-25 from Albuquerque. Take the Placitas exit 242 to go east on NM 165 through Placitas. NM 165 curves around to the

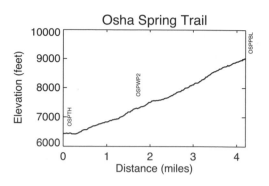

south, and soon becomes a dirt road. Drive a couple of minutes on the dirt portion, and the trailhead is located immediately south of the second one-lane bridge (wp OSPTH). There is a small brown sign on the west side of the road, but it is barely visible from your car.

Description

Osha Spring Trail, a primitive trail, follows an abandoned rock-bed mining road for much of its length. It travels past an old mining operation near Osha Spring. In some places it may be somewhat unclear if you are following the correct route, because there are alternate, parallel branches of the road. However, if you try to keep on the main branch, you will usually come out OK.

You will enjoy handsome views of the mountains and plains to the north and east as well as the eastern slopes of the Sandias along Ohsa Spring Trail. However, the hike uphill is quite a workout. It is also exposed to the sun, and the best season to hike this trail occurs in the spring or fall, when it is cooler.

The trail initially heads in a northerly direction, but after about 0.2 mile it takes a sharp jog back to the south (wp OSPSW). After a little over a mile (wp OSPWP1), the trail takes a distinct turn to the west and opens up a nice view of a canyon to the south and up to the Peñasco Blanco wall of gray rock to the west.

About two miles into the hike, you reach an inviting area for a break (wp OSPWP2). Approaching this spot, the trail is interrupted by twenty to thirty small shrubs that appear to have been planted. Just over the rise beyond this point the trail turns left and goes down into a hidden area. This recess is shaded by tall ponderosa pines and by the ridge that you just walked up. There are large gray "shelf rocks" to sit on for a rest or for lunch.

The scenery along the trail becomes more picturesque beyond this spot. You soon reach a stretch where the trail becomes an eroded dirt road, instead of the rocks that you have been on. In some places the trail becomes indistinct. Farther on, there are a couple of long stretches in which small trees overgrow the trail. You may have to move the limbs apart and keep ducking them for several minutes. Fortunately, the trail is well marked with cairns along the way; these signs reassure that you are still on the trail. Osha Spring Trail passes by the northern rim of Media Canyon (wp OSPWP3) with a view to the south.

Shortly past the overlook, look along the right side of the trail for a pile of rocks cemented together with a stamped medallion on top. This marks an old mining claim (wp LNDMRK). The Landsend barite mine operated in the area long ago. Barite ($BaSO_4$) is a white, crystalline mineral used in paint and as a source of barium in chemicals. The open-pit mine was excavated by a series of bulldozed strips enlarged to pits. The main section of the mine lies north of the trail, about 0.1 mile beyond the marker (wp LNDMIN).

Osha Spring Trail travels over softer soil through thick tree cover and grass about 0.1 mile before you reach the trail end (wp OSPWP4) at the junction with Peñasco Blanco Trail (wp OSPPBL). Osha Spring Trail technically continues to the south for another 0.1 mile, to its junction with Osha Loop Trail (wp OLPOSP).

Osha Spring, from which the trail takes its name, lies north of the junction with Peñasco Blanco Trail (wp OSPPBL). To find the spring, hike north about 0.2 miles on Peñasco Blanco Trail into a clearing. The spring is surrounded by brush, about 250 feet into the clearing and a few feet east of the trail.

To return to your car, retrace your route down Osha Spring Trail. The four-mile hike down the mountain is a lot easier than the long uphill that you've just done.

Crest Trail (No. 130)

Length: 26 miles (total length)
Elevation: 6,240–10,640 feet
Rating: Difficult
See Maps (north to south coverage):
8 (page 71); 5 (page 46);
13 (page 100); 18 (page 118);
17 (page 114)
Driving Instructions: To reach the
north Crest Trail parking
area, drive north on I-25
from Albuquerque. Take the
Placitas exit 242 to go east
on NM 165. The turnoff for

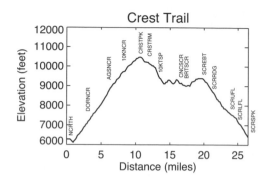

the trail is FR 231, about fifty yards before the five-mile marker. There is
a green street sign that reads Tunnel Spring, plus a group of mailboxes.
Follow the dirt road two miles to the Tunnel Spring trailhead (wp
NCRTH). To access the southern trailhead, take I-40 east from
Albuquerque, then take the south Tijeras exit from I-40. After the exit,
turn left to go under the highway, and then turn right to Canyon Estates.
Follow the residential road to the Crest Trail parking lot (wp SCRSPK).

Description

The Crest Trail (No. 130) extends twenty-six miles from its northern
Tunnel Spring trailhead near Placitas to the southern Canyon Estates
trailhead near Tijeras. All four life zones present in the Sandia
Mountains are encountered along the Crest Trail as it rises from the
Upper Sonoran piñon-juniper landscape at either trailhead to the
Hudsonian zone, confined to about eight hundred acres near Sandia
Crest. Fifteen trails described in this book terminate along the Crest
Trail. Thus, the Crest Trail is not only an important hiking destination
in its own right, but it also is the backbone that combines the Sandia
Mountain's major trails into one connected system. Segments of the
Crest Trail can be used in conjunction with other trails to form loop
hikes. (For more information about the trails that join the Crest Trail,
see their individual trail descriptions.)

Fig. 10. Overlook above Agua Sarca Canyon from the Crest Trail.

The northern trailhead for the Crest Trail is located at Tunnel Spring. At this site, an early mining operation drilled a tunnel into the mountain. It was halted when an underground water source was encountered. The tunnel was blasted shut for safety considerations, but the spring water was piped out, creating Tunnel Spring. A trout hatchery, located just downhill from the current parking lot relied on water from this spring. Also in the area, a metal smelting operation used a beehive-shaped "horno" furnace, which gave rise to the name of the nearby Ojo del Horno Canyon (now referred to as Ojo del Orno Canyon).

The Crest Trail initially heads to the east and passes the entrance to Ojo del Orno Canyon within a hundred yards or so (at the boundary to the Sandia Mountain Wilderness). The Crest Trail makes a broad, gentle 3.3 mile loop to the east and then back west to the head of Ojo del Orno Canyon. The trail passes by remnants of other defunct mines, and old jeep roads cross the trail's path occasionally. An unmaintained trail, Ojo del Orno Route (the next trail described in this book), cuts directly up Ojo del Orno Canyon, intersecting the Crest Trail at the top of the canyon after

0.8 mile of steep climbing (wp DORNCR). I often take this shorter route, cutting off nearly an hour's walk from a long hike.

After passing the upper junction with Ojo del Orno Route (wp DORNCR), the Crest Trail heads west toward the ridgeline and a welcome stone bench. The bench at the top of the ridge provides a good place to rest, with a beautiful view of the Rio Grande Valley to the west. From this point, the Crest Trail continues through two broad switchbacks for another two miles to the intersection with Peñasco Blanco Trail (wp NCRPBL). This portion of the hike has only a slight grade, and makes a pleasant hike through thick oak. From the Peñasco Blanco trailhead, look east to see the large grey limestone formation from which the trail gets its name (*Peñasco blanco* is Spanish for "white bluff"). Hikers will enjoy the view of Palomas Peak to the south from this spot.

The Crest Trail continues west for 0.8 miles across the Cañon Agua Sarca drainage (wp DAGSTR) to the ridgeline (wp AGSNCR). The Crest Trail makes a switchback to the south at the ridge. There is another stone bench at this switchback. The Agua Sarca Route joins the Crest Trail from the north at this spot (see the Agua Sarca Route description, elsewhere in this book).

The Crest Trail travels south for 1.1 miles to another stone bench at the North Del Agua Overlook, offering views across the north fork of Del Agua Canyon. From this location, if you bushwhack south through fifty yards of thick scrub oak, you come out on the north terminus of Ellis Trail (wp ELIEND), described elsewhere. The Crest Trail continues from the overlook through mixed conifers for two-thirds of a mile to the junction with Osha Loop Trail (wp OLPNCR).

The junction with 10K Trail is reached 0.3 miles later at Del Agua Overlook (wp 10KNCR) above the south fork of Del Agua Canyon. The north-facing slope, below the prominent North Sandia Peak, is spectacular in late September, when the changing aspen leaves make it a wash of solid gold. A hike to the peak is described separately under the listing "North Sandia Peak."

From Del Agua Overlook, the Crest Trail continues a steeper uphill climb for almost two miles to Sandia Crest. After passing North Sandia Peak, the trail generally stays just east of the main ridgeline. Along the way there are clearings in the trees to provide magnificent overlooks of the granite rock formations to the west (the Shield, Needle, and Prow, in particular). The trail stays to the east of the fenced area of radio and television towers as it nears Sandia Crest. The trail comes out at the Crest Highway just below the parking area (wp CRSTPK). The convenient access from the Crest Highway makes this location a popular starting point for hikes along the Crest Trail either to the north or to the south.

The Crest Trail picks up again at the southern end of the Crest House, near the restroom facilities. The Crest Spur Trail (No. 84) drops down below the ridgeline from this spot (wp CSPTH) to join La Luz Trail. Continue south along the paved sidewalk to the beginning of the short Crest Nature Trail (No. 98). Rugged Englemann spruce, corkbark fir, Douglas fir, and limber pine of the Hudsonian life zone line the path. Follow the nature trail to its southern end to pick up the Crest Trail, which heads into the woods.

The Crest Trail begins a 1.5 mile course toward the Upper Tram Terminal, which is the most heavily traveled stretch of trail on the mountain. Hundreds of visitors to the mountain (by car or tram) cover this section daily. So, while you won't enjoy much solitude through here, you will meet many excited visitors to the Sandias, some of whom have never been on a mountain trail before.

After less than half a mile (wp CRSKIW) an old gravel road leads to Kiwanis Cabin. This beautiful stone structure, built in the 1930s, sits at the southern end of Kiwanis Meadow. Access to the meadow has been closed for several years to allow it to recover from decades of overuse by visitors. The views from the cabin are spectacular, and well worth the short walk from the Crest Trail. Near the Upper Tram Terminal, the Crest Trail crosses another short nature trail, the Peak Nature Trail (No. 97). The Crest Trail meets the upper La Luz trailhead just north of the Tram Terminal (wp CRSTRM).

The Crest Trail picks up on the south side of the Tram and begins a steady drop in elevation. The first portion of this stretch runs near the main ridgeline to a beautiful overlook above Pino Canyon (wp SCRW5). The trail then makes a couple of broad switchbacks deeper into the forest. About a mile and a half from the Tram Terminal, the Crest Trail meets 10K Trail (its southern end) and Tree Spring Trail (its west end) at the Sandia Mountain Wilderness boundary (wp 10KTSP). Near the ridge, just west of the 10K Trail junction, a spur trail leads to a popular overlook of the canyons below.

The Crest Trail then begins a six-mile stretch of relatively level hiking as it makes its way toward South Sandia Peak. Pino Trail, coming from the west, and Cienega Trail, from the east, meet at the Crest Trail 1.8 miles

Fig. 11. Lush aspen grove north of South Sandia Peak along the Crest Trail.

south of the 10K Trail junction (wp PNOSCR). There is a beautiful scenic overlook about twenty-five yards to the south of the Cienega trailhead. You may have to bushwhack your way through thick brush to reach the rocky overlook at the ridge, but it is worth the effort.

Cañoncito Trail joins the Crest Trail 1.25 miles farther south (wp CNCSCR), as does Bart's Trail after an additional 0.75 mile (wp BRTSCR). Cañoncito and Bart's Trail both reach the main ridgeline from the east, sharing a common trailhead at the bottom. They are popular hiking routes for access to South Sandia Peak. A nice 6.5-mile loop hike can be made by hiking up one of the two trails, then hiking along the Crest Trail to the other's upper trailhead, and then back down the mountain.

The hike south of Bart's Trail is one of my favorites. The Crest Trail passes through one of the nicest aspen groves in the Sandias, and then enters a series of long meadows near South Peak. About a mile south of Bart's Trail, the Crest Trail passes an old wooden shelter (wp SCRW4). Although the regulations for a protected wilderness area prohibit man-made structures, Bear Shelter, as it is called, is allowed to stand as an emergency refuge.

The Crest Trail passes to the east of South Sandia Peak about two miles south of the junction with Bart's Trail. Thick tree cover stands between South Peak and the Crest Trail to the north of the peak. However, as you walk farther south the landscape clears between the Crest Trail and the main ridgeline. To go to South Peak, I usually cut west across the open meadow (for example, at wp SPEAK1, usually marked by a cairn) to pick up a worn trail on the main ridgeline that leads back north to South Peak (wp STHPK). More information about this area is given in the section on "South Sandia Peak."

The Crest Trail reaches the upper terminus of Embudito Trail about 0.7 mile south of South Peak (wp SCREBT). Embudito Trail heads six miles to the northwest, over Deer Pass and down the mountain to the trailhead near Montgomery Blvd. About one hundred yards north of the Embudito Trail junction, the unmaintained CCC Route joins the Crest Trail (wp SCRCCC). CCC is a steep trail that joins the Upper Faulty Trail (just north of the Crest Trail) farther down the mountain. I often take the CCC Route as a shortcut down the mountain from South Peak rather than hiking the Crest Trail's broad loop to the south. Doing so saves over two miles, but be warned that the CCC Route is rugged and hard to follow in some places.

South of Embudito Trail, the Crest Trail begins a steady drop in elevation of almost three thousand feet as it makes its way toward the Canyon Estates trailhead. About one mile south of Embudito Trail, the Crest Trail passes South Sandia Spring (wp SCRSPR), a few feet east of the trail. This spring is usually one of the most reliable in the Sandia Mountains. However, in the recent drought years that we have had, this venerable water source has often been dry. Do not rely on obtaining water from the spring unless you have recent, firsthand knowledge that it has water. (You should always apply appropriate chemical treatment or mechanical filtering to water from any ground sources in the Sandia Mountains.)

About a half mile farther south the Crest Trail leaves the main ridgeline (wp SCRRDG), and begins several broad switchbacks toward the east. Progress down the mountain is slow through this 1.5 mile stretch. The dominant tree cover becomes ponderosa pine as the elevation drops. A little over three miles past the spring, the Crest Trail reaches the junction with Upper Faulty Trail (wp SCRUFL). The lower trailhead for CCC Route is about fifty yards north of this junction (wp CCCUFL), which is usually marked by a large cairn. Continuing east toward Hondo Canyon, the vegetation turns to piñon-juniper forest and the Crest Trail becomes increasingly rocky. The Lower Faulty trailhead (wp SCRLFL) is reached 1.2 miles below the Upper Faulty junction.

The Crest Trail stays near the canyon bottom for the rest of its route. After about a third of a mile, the trail passes a delightful travertine waterfall. A side trail splits off to your right above the falls, just before the Crest Trail crosses from the right to the left side of the streambed. The side trail leads to a cool, shaded area. Water streams (or trickles) down a limestone rock formation above a shallow cave. This is a wonderful place to stop for a snack and water break. Please beware of poison ivy below and above the falls. Interesting large limestone pillars line the Crest Trail near the falls. They are evidence of shifting layers of rock due to geologic faults in the area. A short distance down the Crest Trail is another turnoff to the travertine falls, this one marked by a signpost (wp SCRTRV).

The Crest Trail terminates at the Canyon Estates trailhead one half mile below the falls. The trailhead is marked by a large Forest Service sign with a map of the Sandia Mountain trail system.

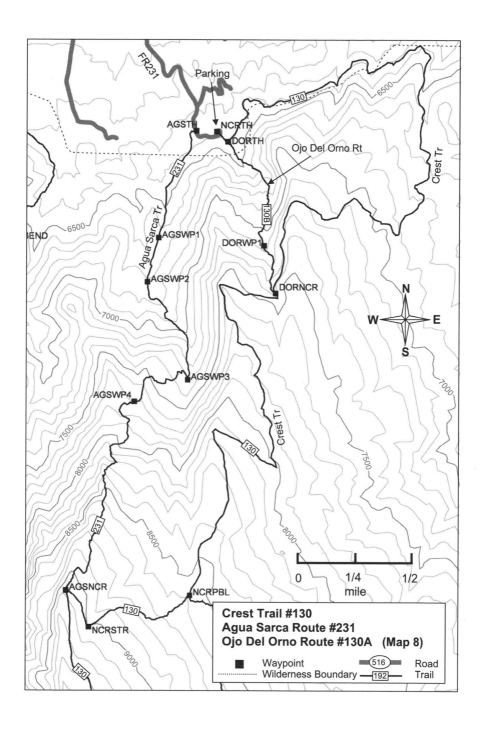

FR231

Parking

130

6500

AGSTH

NCRTH

DORTH

Ojo Del Orno Rt

Crest Tr

231

Agua Sarca Tr

6500

GEND

AGSWP1

130B

DORWP1

AGSWP2

7000

DORNCR

N

W
E

S

AGSWP3

7000

AGSWP4

7500

8000

Crest Tr

130

7500

8500

231

8500

8000

AGSNCR

NCRPBL

130

NCRSTR

9000

130

0   1/4   1/2
         mile

Crest Trail #130
Agua Sarca Route #231
Ojo Del Orno Route #130A   (Map 8)

■ Waypoint   516   Road
...... Wilderness Boundary 192   Trail

Ojo del Orno Route (No. 130B)

Length: 0.8 mile (one way)
Elevation: 6,400–7,410 feet
Rating: Difficult
See Map: 8 (page 71)
Driving Instructions: To reach the north Crest Trail parking area, drive north on I-25 from Albuquerque. Take the Placitas exit 242 to go east on NM 165. The turnoff for the trail is FR 231, about fifty yards west of the five-

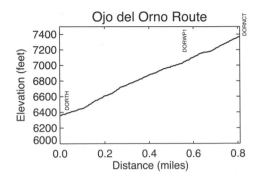

mile marker. There is a green street sign that reads Tunnel Spring and a group of mailboxes. Drive south on FR 231 for two miles to the Tunnel Spring (Crest Trail) parking area marked by signs (wp NCRTH).

Description

Ojo del Orno Route is a steep but quick route to get to higher elevations in the northern part of the Sandias. The name should properly be Ojo del Horno, meaning Eye of the Furnace, but it has commonly been spelled "del Orno" on maps for many years. The name recalls the beehive-shaped furnace ("horno") from mining and smelter activity in the area of Tunnel Spring.

Ojo del Orno Route goes up Ojo del Orno Canyon just east of the Tunnel Spring trailhead. It meets the Crest Trail near the top of this canyon, elevation 7,410 feet. Ojo del Orno Route provides a direct route to the greener areas of the Crest Trail, bypassing a 3.3 mile broad loop to the east. It is a rough and rocky trail, and it is not part of the Forest Service system of maintained trails. Nonetheless it is popular with many hikers who want a more direct path up the mountain. (I often hike this route myself rather than the longer Crest Trail swing to the east.)

To find Ojo del Orno Route, begin hiking from the Tunnel Spring trail-head (wp NCRTH). The turnoff to Ojo del Orno Route is just a few feet past a large Forest Service sign marking the Sandia Mountain Wilderness boundary (wp DORTH). A few feet before the streambed, the Ojo del Orno Route heads off to the south.

It is generally easy to follow the trail its entire length. Ojo del Orno Route is steep and rugged, and it is a great workout. It is somewhat less than a mile hike up the canyon to reach the intersection with the Crest Trail (wp DORNCR).

If you are hiking down the Crest Trail, the turnoff to Ojo del Orno Route can be a little hard to spot. As you are hiking down the Crest Trail, it turns sharply east, leaving the ridgeline overlooking Agua Sarca Canyon. (There is a stone bench at this turn, elevation about 7,600 feet.) The turnoff to Ojo del Orno Route is 0.2 mile past this bench and overlook. The Crest Trail makes a sharp inside turn as it crosses a streambed running down Ojo del Orno Canyon. Ojo del Orno Route drops down and to the left about fifty yards past the streambed (wp DORNCR). This junction is usually marked by a cairn.

Agua Sarca Route (No. 231)

Length: 3 miles (one way)
Elevation: 6,350–9,040 feet
Rating: Difficult
See Map: 8 (page 71)
Driving Instructions: To find the Agua Sarca Route, drive north on I-25 from Albuquerque. Take the Placitas exit 242 to go east on NM 165. Take the turnoff for FR 231 about fifty yards before the five-mile marker on this highway. At the turnoff, there is a green street sign that reads Tunnel Spring and a group of mailboxes. Follow the dirt road almost two miles to a sign for the Agua Sarca trailhead on the west side of the road, and a parking area to the left (wp AGSTH).

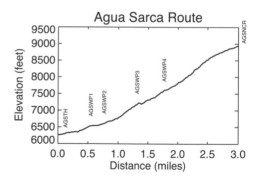

Description
The Agua Sarca Route is not an officially maintained trail in the Sandia Mountains, although it does have a recognized trail number (No. 231). As

with any of the unmaintained routes, the trail may be hard to follow, or disappear altogether at some points. You should only take one of these routes if you are familiar with navigating rough territory using a map and compass (or GPS), in case you become lost.

The route generally follows an old jeep trail for the first three quarters of a mile. It heads up a steep slope to a saddle point (wp AGSWP1), then drops into Agua Sarca Canyon (the name is Spanish for "blue water"). There is an important "Y" in the trail 0.2 mile later (wp AGSWP2); the **left** branch is the correct route. (Unfortunately, the brush is very thick at this split in the trail, and it may be hard to spot the left branch. It will be tempting to go straight ahead, up a streambed. Although it appears to be a nice route, that branch goes nowhere.) Going left, you will find an easy-to-follow trail. From there, the trail begins a steep section that is more of a traditional trail, that is, a narrow trail cutting through tree cover.

You will come upon a distinct "T" in the trail (wp AGSWP3) about a mile and a half into the hike. The left branch continues to parallel the stream, but is quite overgrown. The correct path is the well-worn route to the right.

Following the right branch of the trail, you are eventually led to a huge pile of rocks. At one time this may have been a shelter of some sort; it certainly is a noticeable landmark (wp AGSWP4). The trail used to disappear at this spot. However, around 2000 the route was cleared and extended all the way to the Crest Trail.

The trail continues south climbing through some steep terrain. At some places (especially some rocky places near the top) the trail is hard to see. However, there are many cairns (that you have to look closely for) to mark the way. At about 7,600' the east slope rocks have turned white or yellow, probably because of long-term spring activity.

The trail joins the Crest Trail (wp AGSNCR) at a sharp switchback along the ridgeline. There is a welcome stone bench at this point to rest after your long hike uphill.

Extending your hike: From the junction with the Crest Trail, you may carefully retrace your steps down the steep Agua Sarca Route. However, I think a better alternative is to hike down the Crest Trail and Ojo del Orno Canyon, making a loop. Taking this alternate route down the mountain adds about 1.2 miles to your hike over the more direct path down Agua Sarca Route.

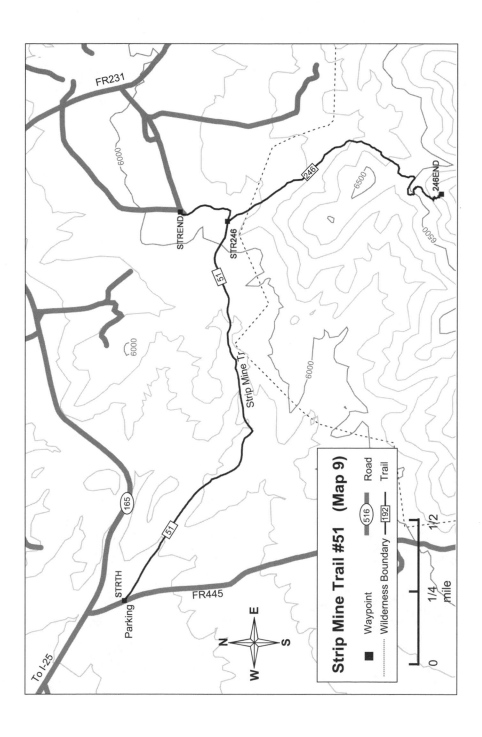

Strip Mine Trail #51 (Map 9)

Legend:
- ■ Waypoint
- .... Wilderness Boundary
- 516 Road
- 192 Trail

FR231

6000

246

6500

246END

6500

STREND

STR246

51

51

Strip Mine Tr

6000

6000

165

51

STRTH

FR445

Parking

To I-25

N E S W

0   1/4   1/2
mile

Strip Mine Trail (No. 51)

Length: 1.8 miles (one way)
Elevation: 5,660–6,040 feet
Rating: Moderate
See Map: 9 (page 75)
Driving Instructions: To find Strip Mine Trail, drive north on I-25 from Albuquerque. Take the Placitas exit 242 to go east on NM 165. After about three miles, turn south onto FR 455. The parking area for the trail is about one hundred yards south of NM 165 (wp STRTH).

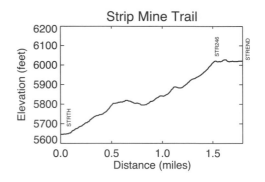

Description

Strip Mine Trail, a rough and exposed trail, follows an old jeep road past an abandoned strip mine from which the trail gets its name. The trail is

Fig. 12. Rolling hills along Strip Mine Trail.

shared by hikers, mountain bikers, and horseback riders. The hike is moderate and relatively flat, but I recommend that you try this trail early in the morning or during the winter months; the direct exposure to the sun and lack of shade can make it a very hot hike.

The trail goes up and down through small gullies, and passes a small strip mine to the north. The exposed earth below the top soil is red and quite striking. The route also passes through junipers, low scrub brush, and cactus, which are about the only vegetation in the area.

After about a mile and a half walk, the hike reaches a fork in the trail (wp STR246). Another trail (No. 246, see below) heads south from here, but take the left branch to reach the east trailhead for Strip Mine Trail, about a quarter of a mile from this junction. The trail comes out on a dirt road (wp STREND) that serves local residents.

Extending your hike: I enjoy hiking south on Trail 246 (from wp STR246), which leads to higher elevations and some greenery. Trail 246 goes back and forth a few times through a fence marking the wilderness boundary and begins some modest elevation gain. The trail makes its way toward a small peak (7,011' elevation), but begins to peter out before reaching the top (wp 246END). If you decide to bushwhack your way to the top, you will see rewarding views of the area.

Del Agua Route (No. 248)

Length: 1.8 miles (one way)
Elevation: 5,960–7,020 feet
Rating: Moderate
See Map: 10 (page 79)
Driving Instructions: To reach the trailhead, drive north on I-25 from Albuquerque. Take the Placitas exit 242 to go east on NM 165. After about three miles, turn south onto FR 455.

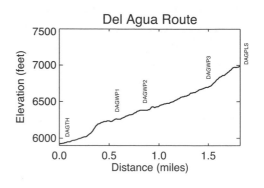

It is about a 2.5-mile drive on the dirt road to reach the Del Agua trailhead (wp DAGTH), marked by signs.

Description

Del Agua Route heads south from the trailhead and gains a slight elevation along the slope to the east. Upon reaching Del Agua Canyon, the trail turns eastward. (*Del agua* is Spanish for "of the water," named for the canyon's spring and small stream.) After half a mile or so, the trail drops into the canyon bottom along the streambed (wp DAGWP1). The trail is overgrown and a little hard to discern at some places along the way. At 0.9 mile into the hike, there is a significant split in the canyon (wp DAGWP2). Take the left branch to follow the Del Agua Route; this branch follows the north fork of Del Agua Canyon. (The branch to the right leads up the south fork of Del Agua Canyon. Piedra Lisa Trail enters the canyon south fork about 2.5 miles from its north trailhead, wp PLSWP2.) About 0.6 mile farther on Del Agua Route, the canyon splits again (wp DAGWP3), and you want to take the left branch, which leads up to Piedra Lisa Trail.

On the last portion of Del Agua Route, the trail follows a sandy arroyo bottom through ponderosa pine cover. Almost two miles from the trailhead, Del Agua Route intersects Piedra Lisa Trail (wp DAGPLS). The intersection is not marked with a sign. However, Piedra Lisa Trail is well worn and there is usually a rock cairn next to the junction. (This point is hard to miss when coming up Del Agua Canyon as you've done. However, if you were hiking on Piedra Lisa Trail, it would be easy to overlook the turnoff to the lesser worn Del Agua Route.) This junction marks the end of Del

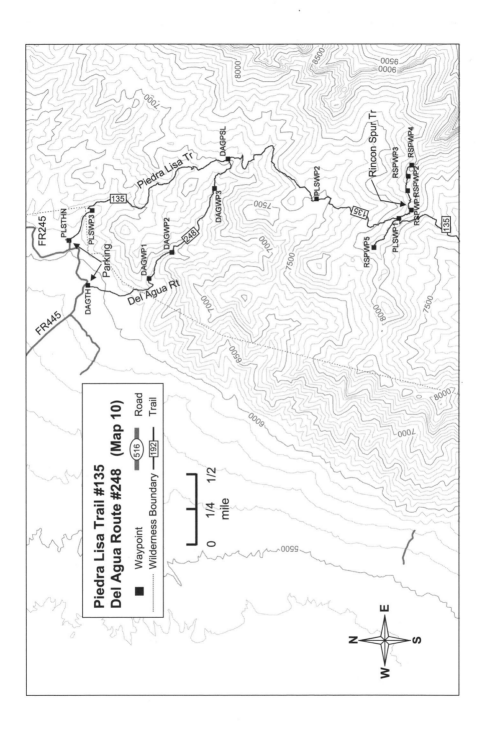

Piedra Lisa Trail #135
Del Agua Route #248   (Map 10)

■ Waypoint
.... Wilderness Boundary

◁516▷ Road
—192— Trail

0   1/4   1/2
mile

N
W · E · S

Agua Route. To return to your car, either retrace your steps down Del Agua Canyon or hike north on Piedra Lisa Trail (see below).

Extending your hike: From this point, you can head south if you are interested in seeing more of Piedra Lisa Trail, or turn north on Piedra Lisa Trail toward your car. From the junction with Del Agua Route (wp DAGPLS) northward, the 1.75 miles along Piedra Lisa Trail are quite steep in places, with bare hillsides and little shade. There are plenty of loose rocks on the steep trail, so good hiking boots will give you secure footing. The trail ends at a water storage tank. Follow the arroyo bed northwest to the parking area (wp PLSTHN), then walk about a half mile west and south on Forest Road 445 to your car at the Del Agua parking area (wp DAGTH).

La Luz Trail (No. 137)

Length: 7.5 miles (one way)
Elevation: 7,040–10,250 feet
Rating: Difficult
See Map: 6 (page 52)
Driving Instructions: Take Tramway Boulevard one mile north of the turnoff to the Tram. Turn east onto FR 333, and follow the paved road about two miles to La Luz Trail parking lot (wp LLZTH) near the Juan Tabo Picnic Ground.

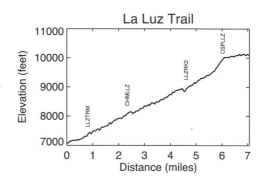

Description

La Luz Trail is the best known trail in the Sandia Mountains. It is also one of the most challenging. It takes the hiker from hot desert landscape to cool Canadian forest. The length (7.5 miles each way) and elevation gain (around 3,200 vertical feet) make La Luz Trail a difficult but rewarding outing. Before setting out on this hike, you should be well prepared with plenty of water, food, sunscreen, and a rain jacket in case of a sudden change in weather. Each year, search and rescue teams hunt for inexperienced hikers who wander off La Luz Trail and become stranded or lost. La Luz Trail is an extremely well-traveled and distinct trail its full length. Please pay attention and follow the well-worn path.

La luz is Spanish for "the light." Two proposed explanations of the name exist. A mining operation was begun in the 1920s, not far from one of the upper switchbacks along the present La Luz Trail. It may be that the mine was called La Luz because the city lights of Albuquerque were visible from the mine (and the lights of a cabin at the mine were also visible from the city). Other locations in New Mexico called La Luz are named in honor of *Nuestra Señora de la Luz*, Spanish for "Our Lady of the Light" (the Virgin Mary).

La Luz is a long, strenuous trail, and often people choose to hike it in one direction only (rather than making the fifteen-mile round trip). This can be done in several ways, usually taking advantage of the Sandia Peak Aerial Tramway. For example, you can leave a car at the base of the Tram, then hike up La Luz from the Juan Tabo trailhead, finish at the Upper Tram Terminal, and ride the Tram down. This loop can just as easily be done in the opposite direction, that is, ride up, and hike down to the La Luz trailhead. Alternately, you can take advantage of Tramway Trail, which joins La Luz about one mile from the La Luz trailhead. For example, from the Lower Tram Terminal you can hike 2.5 miles north on Tramway Trail to La Luz Trail, then continue on La Luz Trail to the Upper Tram Terminal and ride down (or do the whole circuit in the opposite direction).

At the Juan Tabo trailhead there is a large parking area with restroom facilities. This lot is usually full on weekends, and a Forest Service attendant is often on duty to help with traffic flow and to answer questions. Just up a set of concrete steps to the east is a large Forest Service sign showing a map of the entire Sandia Mountain trail system, and giving other hiking and safety information.

The hike begins through an impressive boulder field and beautiful cacti. La Luz Trail heads south with a modest uphill grade that it maintains most of its length. Early in the hike you will enjoy great views of lower Juan Tabo Canyon to the west. The trail makes a few switchbacks to gain elevation as it approaches a small canyon and streambed, passing a few rock retaining walls along the way. One mile into the hike you reach the junction with Tramway Trail (wp LLZTRM), marked by a sign. The right branch at this intersection would take you to the Lower Tram Terminal, 2.5 miles away. However, to continue up La Luz Trail, take the left branch.

Fig. 13. The Thumb as seen from La Luz Trail.

La Luz Trail begins a long series of switchbacks traversing the southwest-facing slope. This stretch of trail is hot and exposed to the direct sun. Around 2.2 miles into the hike, the switchbacks end for the moment as the trail rounds a ridge into Chimney Canyon, heading east. Impressive rock cliffs and the Sandia Crest radio towers loom overhead. La Luz Trail crosses a lush tree-covered streambed at a sharp right turn in the trail, 0.2 miles later. (Many lost hikers wander off the trail here, heading up the overgrown stream into Chimney Canyon. The proper route is straight across the stream to a well-worn trail leading south and out of the tree cover.)

Spectacular views of La Cueva Canyon come into view a short distance later. The trail enters tall ponderosa pine coverage 3.25 miles into the hike, at around 8,400 feet in elevation. The trail makes several switchbacks along the ridge between Chimney Canyon to the north and La Cueva Canyon to the south, providing overlooks at each turnaround along the way. Beautiful views of the Thumb rock formation open up as the trail heads south. There is a scenic overlook just to the right of the trail 4.3 miles into the hike, with views into La Cueva Canyon. The trail begins a short downhill section across rough granite to reach the base of a rockslide (wp LLZRK2) and the start of the most challenging portion of the hike. A warning sign notes that the trail may be dangerous and impassable beyond this point in winter.

La Luz Trail begins a series of switchbacks up the south face of La Cueva Canyon on the talus slope beneath the Thumb. The trail moves back and forth across rough granite that makes for slow going on the lower portion. Much of the hike up the rockslides is exposed to the direct sun. The trail makes fifteen switchbacks across the rocky terrain, gaining about nine hundred feet in elevation over about a mile and a half distance. As you cross the eighth switchback, keep an eye out for Donald Duck Rock, a cute landmark along the way. As you cross the wide granite boulder field walking east you will pass a significant rock formation, a "fin" perhaps 50 feet high to your left (wp DDUCK, elevation about 9,660'). Look skyward at a compass bearing of 200° (just west of south) to see the head and bills of the famous duck in silhouette. Donald Duck Rock is on a formation just east of the Thumb.

At the top of the rock slides (wp LLZRK1), the trail switches to softer ground on the western slope of the canyon shortly before reaching a saddle point, which is the junction with the Crest Spur Trail (wp CSPLLZ), about 6.2 miles into the hike. The Crest Spur Trail heads 0.7 miles to Sandia Crest, going north from this junction. There have been a number of different trail routes for La Luz over the decades. Traditionally, La Luz Trail extended to Sandia Crest; purists would argue that it should do so today. However, the short segment heading to the Crest from the saddle point is now called the Crest Spur Trail. La Luz Trail itself continues a little over a mile, going south from this junction to the Upper Tram Terminal.

As discussed above, many people ride the Sandia Peak Tramway back down the mountain. The alternative is a long, but beautiful, trip back down La Luz Trail.

Piedra Lisa Trail (No. 135)

Length: 5.7 miles (one way)
Elevation: 6,030–8,150 feet
Rating: Moderate
See Map: 10 (page 79); 11 (page 86)
Driving Instructions: To find the south trailhead, take Tramway Blvd. one mile north of the turnoff to the Tram, and turn east onto FR 333. After two

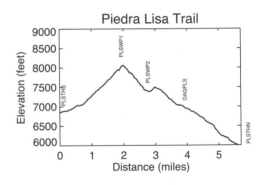

miles, pass the turnoff to La Luz Trail (that direction is marked FR 333), and continue straight ahead, on the dirt FR 333D. The dirt road makes a right turn around a corner, and leads back to the Piedra Lisa Trail parking lot (wp PLSTHS). For the north trailhead, drive north on I-25 from Albuquerque. Take the Placitas exit 242 to go east on NM 165. After about three miles, turn south onto FR 455 and drive two miles to the trailhead (wp PLSTHN).

Note: The area to the east of Piedra Lisa Trail (south of the Rincon) is closed to protect sensitive wildlife areas between March 1 and August 15 every year.

Description
Piedra Lisa Trail runs from its southern trailhead just north of the La Luz Trail, over the Rincon Ridge, to its northern trailhead near the Placitas

highway, NM 165. The southern portion of the trail is quite popular and receives traffic year round. Because the trailheads are so far apart, I usually take the southern and northern halves on separate hikes, rather than shuttling cars to leave one at each end or making a long round trip (which requires climbing over the Rincon Ridge twice on an eleven-mile hike).

From the southern parking lot (wp PLSTHS), walk 0.4 mile along the dirt road to reach the beginning of Piedra Lisa Trail (wp PLSWP4). The trail goes up a rise and then drops into Juan Tabo Canyon after a short distance. At the low point in the trail (wp FLETH) is a junction with two canyons coming down from the east, Waterfall Canyon (the southern canyon) and upper Juan Tabo Canyon (the northern one). Three hiking routes head into these areas. Fletcher Trail heads northeast into upper Juan Tabo Canyon. Another rough route heads about a mile into Waterfall Canyon to a nice waterfall (that hike requires significant bush-whacking along the way). Movie Trail heads up the ridge separating the two canyons. As noted above, this area east of Piedra Lisa Trail is officially closed to the public between March 1 and August 15 every year, to protect wildlife.

Piedra Lisa Trail continues north from the canyon bottom along an especially beautiful stretch. The trail travels up Juan Tabo Ridge separating upper Juan Tabo Canyon to the east and the broad lower Juan Tabo Canyon to the west. Along the way there are splendid views into the canyons on both sides, as well as views of the granite rock formations of the mountain's western face (for example, the Shield, Needle, Prow, and UNM Spire).

Two miles into the hike, Piedra Lisa Trail reaches the top of the Rincon, a long ridgeline running west from the base of the Shield. Signs mark the top of the ridge (wp PLSWP1), pointing the way for the continuation of Piedra Lisa Trail to the north. The Rincon Spur Trail bisects Piedra Lisa Trail at this point and runs along the ridge to the east and to the west; this route is described elsewhere in the book. When hiking only the southern portion of Piedra Lisa Trail, I usually hike the Rincon Spur Trail and then return to my car from here.

Piedra Lisa Trail continues north from the Rincon and drops steeply into the south fork of Del Agua Canyon. The hiking is easy and enjoyable through pleasant ponderosa pine, piñon, and juniper forest. A little less than a mile north of the Rincon the trail drops into the sandy canyon bottom. A sign marks the halfway point of Piedra Lisa Trail here. The trail becomes indistinct in places, so pay close attention as you pass through

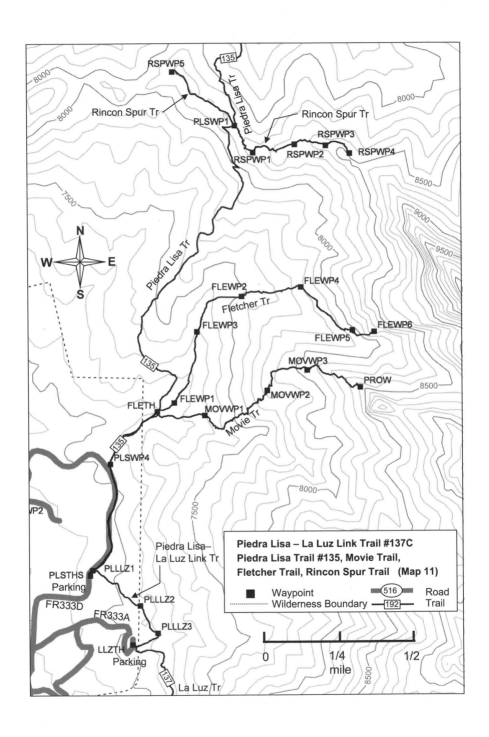

RSPWP5

135

8000

8000

Piedra Lisa Tr

Rincon Spur Tr

PLSWP1

Rincon Spur Tr

RSPWP3

RSPWP4

RSPWP2

RSPWP1

8000

8500

7500

N

W   E

S

9000

9500

Piedra Lisa Tr

FLEWP2

Fletcher Tr

FLEWP4

FLEWP3

8000

FLEWP6

FLEWP5

135

MOVWP3

PROW

8500

FLETH

FLEWP1

MOVWP2

MOVWP1

Movie Tr

135

PLSWP4

8000

P2

7500

Piedra Lisa–
La Luz Link Tr

PLLLZ1

PLSTHS
Parking

FR333D

PLLLZ2

FR333A

PLLLZ3

LLZTH
Parking

137

La Luz Tr

8500

Piedra Lisa – La Luz Link Trail #137C
Piedra Lisa Trail #135, Movie Trail,
Fletcher Trail, Rincon Spur Trail   (Map 11)

■ Waypoint   516   Road
.... Wilderness Boundary   192   Trail

0   1/4   1/2
                 mile

Fig. 14. Views of the Shield, Prow, and Needle (left to right) from Piedra Lisa Trail.

this area. In 2002 Sandia Pueblo bought the surrounding 160-acre parcel of land, which had been a private property inholding for decades. The land purchase was part of the pueblo's effort to settle its longstanding Sandia Mountain land claim with the federal government.

Piedra Lisa Trail continues north, rising out of the canyon bottom. The trail soon passes over a saddle point and enters the north fork of Del Agua Canyon. About a mile later the trail passes the junction with Del Agua Route, No. 248 (wp DAGPLS). That hiking route travels up the north fork of Del Agua Canyon from a trailhead about one half mile west of Piedra Lisa Trail's north trailhead. (See the section "Extending your hike," below.)

About a quarter mile north of this junction Piedra Lisa Trail enters another canyon on its last stretch. In many places the path is quite steep, with bare hillsides and little shade. There are plenty of loose rocks on the steep trail, so be careful of your footing. The trail gets its name from the rock in this area (*Piedra lisa* is Spanish for "smooth rock.") Near the mouth of the canyon the trail passes a water-holding tank and a large Forest Service trail sign. Follow the trail up the arroyo to the parking area (wp PLSTHN).

Extending your hike: From the Rincon ridge (wp PLSWP1) you can hike to the east or to the west along the Rincon Spur Trail to some rugged territory and beautiful views; see the separate discussion of the Rincon Spur Trail for more details. From the northern portion of the mountain, a three-mile loop can be made by hiking up Del Agua Route and then down Piedra Lisa Trail.

Piedra Lisa–La Luz Link (No. 137C)

Length: 0.5 mile (one way)
Elevation: 6,960–7,200 feet
Rating: Easy
See Map: 11 (page 86)
Driving Instructions: Take Tramway Boulevard one mile north of the turnoff to the Tram, and turn east onto FR 333. After two miles, pass the turnoff to La Luz Trail (that direction is marked FR 333), and continue straight ahead, on the dirt FR 333D. The dirt road makes a right turn around a corner, and leads back to the Piedra Lisa Trail parking lot (wp PLSTHS). Alternatively, follow FR 333 to the La Luz Trail parking area (wp LLZTH) to hike this trail from its southeast end.

Description
The Piedra Lisa–La Luz Link forms a short connecting trail between two popular west-side hiking destinations. This trail serves two purposes that I can see. It is a short, easy hike through the western foothills for those in search of a nice evening's walk, for example. The trail also serves to link the parking areas for Piedra Lisa and La Luz trails. The parking area at La Luz Trail is often full on weekends. A hiker may wish to park at the nearby Piedra Lisa Trail lot and walk the half mile to the La Luz trailhead via this linking trail.

The trailhead for this short trail is easy to find. As you walk out of the north end of the Piedra Lisa parking lot, go up to the dirt road. Straight in front of you (across the dirt road) lies a worn trail leading up the embankment (wp PLLLZ1). This is the northwest trailhead for the Piedra Lisa–La Luz Link, which makes its way southwest. After 0.25 mile, the trail heads south across an arroyo (wp PLLLZ2), and the turnoff is easy to miss. The trail crosses another narrower streambed a short while later (wp PLLLZ3), where it is again easy to lose track of the trail. (I almost always lose the trail at this spot when hiking it in the opposite direction.) The trail passes a large, ground-level concrete holding tank about fifty yards before the trail ends at the northeast corner of the La Luz Trail parking lot (wp LLZTH).

La Cueva Trail (No. 83)

Length: 0.3 mile (one way)
Elevation: 6,500–6,700 feet
Rating: Easy
See Map: 12 (page 91)
Driving Instructions: Take Tramway Boulevard (NM 556) one mile north of the turnoff to the Sandia Peak Aerial Tramway, and turn east onto FR 333. After crossing the second cattle guard (0.3 mile), turn right on FR 333B and follow the main asphalt road for one mile. Turn right as the road going east ends, and park in a small lot fifty yards to the south at the trailhead for La Cueva Trail, marked by a sign (wp LCVTH). The area is closed each day from sunset to sunrise. Note that FR 333B is usually closed by a locked gate in winter.

Description

La Cueva Trail is a short connecting trail between the La Cueva Picnic Ground and Tramway Trail. The La Cueva Picnic Ground features many stone picnic tables and structures built by master stoneworkers in the Civilian Conservation Corps during the 1930s. The structures were constructed to blend seamlessly into the surrounding rocks and trees. A beautiful stone pavilion stands just to the southwest of the trailhead. The picnic ground is listed in the New Mexico Registry of Historic Places. *La cueva* is Spanish for "the cave," and the area was probably named for a specific cave in La Cueva Canyon to the east.

From the parking area La Cueva Trail heads east along a worn old path lined with cactus, grass, chamisa, rock, and pampas grass. This short trail is notable for its beautiful silhouette views to the northeast of the Shield, North Sandia Peak, and the Needle. After 0.3 mile the trail meets Tramway Trail (wp TRMLCV). A distinct trail continues eastward toward La Cueva Canyon, but this spot is the official end of La Cueva Trail.

Extending your hike: You can hike south on Tramway Trail for less than a half mile to visit Jaral Cabin, the ruins of an old Forest Ranger Station near the junction of Tramway Trail and Rozamiento Trail (wp ROZTRM). For a more strenuous outing, continue along the crude trail into La Cueva Canyon. You will soon be scrambling up rocks and picking your way back into a rugged section of the Sandias. In early years La Luz Trail went up the lower portion of La Cueva Canyon, and traces of the trail are evident today. If you travel into the canyon, make sure you don't venture into terrain that you are not equipped to handle.

Rozamiento Trail (No. 208)

Length: 0.6 mile (one way)
Elevation: 6,250–6,500 feet
Rating: Easy
See Map: 12 (page 91)
Driving Instructions: Take Tramway Boulevard to the turnoff as if you were driving to the lower Tram Terminal. Take the second left onto Juniper Hills Drive, and follow it north and west until you run into Spring Creek Lane. (If you accidentally divert to Rock Ridge Drive from Juniper Hills, take heart. It eventually turns back into Juniper Hills, which will run into Spring Creek Lane.) When Spring Creek Lane dips to cross a broad sandy arroyo, park your car at the dirt lot on the east side of the road (wp ROZPK).

Description
Rozamiento in Spanish means "friction." Rozamiento Canyon is sometimes used by experienced rock climbers. In the canyon there are huge slabs of granite, some quite steep, some canted to the left or right. With skill, the climber can walk up such faces by employing as much friction

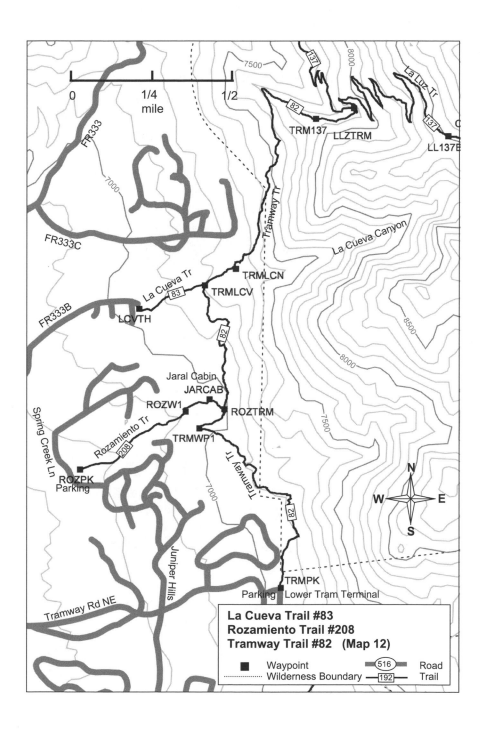

La Cueva Trail #83
Rozamiento Trail #208
Tramway Trail #82   (Map 12)

■ Waypoint   ▬▬516▬▬ Road
⋯⋯⋯⋯ Wilderness Boundary —■192■— Trail

as possible, a so-called friction climb. My guess is that the name is relatively recent, and has this origin. The trail is also known as Jaral Cabin Trail, and it is listed as such on some maps. In New Mexico, the word *jara* refers to a type of willow; Jaral Canyon is surely a variant of that Spanish word referring to trees in the area. For good measure, the trail is also sometimes called Spring Creek Trail, the name listed on a sign at the intersection with Tramway Trail. There is a spring and creek bed near the cabin ruins.

Rozamiento Trail passes near a number of residential properties, so please respect the privacy of the homeowners. This short trail follows a chamisa-filled arroyo most of its length. Rozamiento Trail also doubles as an equestrian route. This trail provides an alternate route for access to Tramway Trail, rather than starting from the Tram parking lot.

From the parking area, the trail heads east and up the broad arroyo. This is a well-traveled trail and easy to follow its short (0.6 mile) length. After about a ten-minute walk up the arroyo, the trail lifts out of the streambed (wp ROZW1) and veers north. A short distance later, the ruins of Jaral Cabin (wp JARCAB) come into view. Only the stone foundation of this old cabin remains. The cabin is thought to have been built by the CCC in the 1930s, and was used by the Forest Service up to the early 1960s. An intermittent stream originates near the ruins of Jaral Cabin.

Rozamiento Trail ends about a hundred yards farther east, where it intersects with Tramway Trail (wp ROZTRM). There, a sign points to the north for Tramway Trail and back down to the west for Spring Creek Trail (one of the other names for Rozamiento Trail). Return to your car (wp ROZPK) down the route that you have just come up, or explore Tramway Trail in either direction while you are in the area.

Extending your hike: For more rugged exploration, follow Tramway Trail a couple of hundred yards south of Jaral Cabin to pick up the streambed again. Follow the streambed east into Rozamiento Canyon while keeping an eye out for crude trails. Do *not* attempt to climb any of the rock formations in the canyon unless you have training.

Tramway Trail (No. 82)

Length: 2.5 miles (one way)
Elevation: 6,460–7,400 feet
Rating: Moderate
See Map: 12 (page 91)
Driving Instructions: To find the trailhead, drive to the (lower) Tram terminal via Tramway Blvd. Pay the parking fee on your way past the guard station at the Tram. The trailhead is located at the northeast corner of the upper parking area (wp TRMPK).

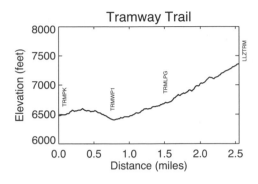

Description

Tramway Trail furnishes a good hike in the winter months when the upper mountain is difficult to hike because of snow. The trail has little shade at this low elevation, and because it faces west it can be a hot hike in warmer months. Tramway Trail begins at the base of the Tram and runs north, joining La Luz Trail. It is probably most commonly used as a connector to La Luz Trail by people who park at the Tram, ride the Tram to the top of the mountain, and then hike down La Luz (or make the loop in the opposite direction).

Tramway Trail passes near private residences along most of its length. It has been rerouted higher in elevation from its original path to stay farther away from the homes. Please do your best to follow the signs and keep on the path.

About a mile into the hike you pass a sign pointing the way to Spring Creek (wp ROZTRM). You can see the ruins of an old ranger cabin (Jaral Cabin) just down the trail to the west (wp JARCAB). The cabin, most likely built in the 1930s by the CCC, was used by Forest Rangers as a base to monitor the western side of the Sandia Mountains until the early 1960s. The Rozamiento Trail (also know as Jaral Cabin Trail or Spring Creek Trail) slopes downhill from this point.

About a half mile farther north is a signpost pointing the way to La Cueva Picnic Ground (wp TRMLCV). This trail is only one-third of a mile long. The picnic facilities in the area were built in the 1930s by the Civilian

Conservation Corps. La Cueva Trail serves primarily as a connector to access Tramway Trail from La Cueva Picnic Ground.

Tramway Trail continues north and almost immediately crosses the streambed of La Cueva Canyon. In typical years, a stream reaches the trail crossing before soaking into the sand. After crossing La Cueva Canyon the trail climbs gradually and crosses a ridge into the La Luz drainage and joins La Luz Trail at the bottom of a long series of switchbacks (wp LLZTRM).

Foothills Trail (No. 365)

Length: 13 miles (total length)
Elevation: 5,860–6,660 feet
Rating: Easy
See Maps (north to south coverage): 22 (page 146); 15 (page 106); 24 (page 156); 25 (page 160)
Driving Instructions: To find the northern trailhead, drive to the (lower) Tram terminal via Tramway Blvd. You will have

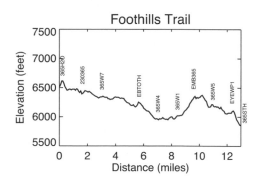

to pay a parking fee on your way past the guard station at the Tram. The trailhead is located at the southeast corner of the upper parking area (wp 365NTH). To reach the southern trailhead, turn east on Encantado from Tramway Boulevard (0.4 mile north of Central). Follow Encantado for 0.6 mile, then turn right on Manor Ct., then make a quick left on Hilldale, then a quick right on Camino de la Sierra. Follow Camino de la Sierra for 0.4 mile and park at the south end of the fenced Albuquerque Open Space area on your left (wp 365STH). Numerous other access points for the Foothills Trail are also listed below.

Description

The Foothills Trail (No. 365) parallels the western foothills of the Sandia Mountains. It stretches from the Sandia Peak Aerial Tramway lower terminal to the Open Space Area just north of I-40. The trail is primarily used by mountain bike riders. However, because of its close proximity to Albuquerque and ease of access, it serves as a convenient hiking route year round. In addition to the north and south trailheads described above, you may also pick up Trail 365 from parking areas near the east end of Montgomery (Embudito trailhead), Comanche, Candelaria (Open Space parking lot), Menaul, Indian School (Embudo trailhead), and Copper boulevards.

The Foothills Trail begins with a short, steep climb from the southeast corner of the Tram parking lot toward two large water tanks (wp 365H2O) to the south. The trail winds through high desert landscape with the Sandia foothills to the east and housing developments to the west. After 1.75 miles the trail approaches the Elena Gallegos / Albert G. Simms Park (wp 230365). This 640-acre Open Space area is popular with walkers and bike riders. The Foothills Trail itself stays just to the west of the park boundary, but along the way it intersects with several numbered trails coming from the Open Space. Foothills Trail crosses the asphalt road that leads to the Open Space parking area just west of the guard station (wp 365W7) about 1.4 miles farther south. The trail continues south through gently rolling terrain for another 2.5 miles to the Embudito Trail parking lot (wp EBTOTH).

Fig. 15. U-Mound from the Open Space Area in the southwest foothills.

Trail 365 is interrupted here, stopped by the neighboring housing areas that have pushed into the foothills. The trail picks up again about a mile and a half south, at a small entrance to the Albuquerque Open Space at the east end of Comanche Blvd. Mountain bikers (or walkers) wishing to continue from the Embudito trailhead to this next segment heading south should go west on Trailhead Rd., then go south on Glenwood Hills Dr. past Montgomery Blvd. Glenwood Hills Dr. becomes Camino de la Sierra (at Sunset Rd.). Follow Camino de la Sierra south to Comanche Blvd. and the entrance to the Open Space area (wp 365W4). The Foothills Trail continues south, running just to the east of the neighboring houses.

Continuing south, after about 0.75 mile the Foothills Trail passes the mouth of Piedra Lisa Canyon and another Open Space parking area (wp PLCYPK). The canyon is notable for a large gray rock formation near the entrance, which looks like a natural dam. The canyon area is crisscrossed with dozens of faint trails, making it a great area to explore. This area is also discussed in the section titled "Piedra Lisa Canyon" in this book. About a half mile farther south, the Foothills Trail passes through an Open Space picnic area just east of the parking lot at the end of Menaul Blvd. (wp 365W1).

The trail then begins a gentle uphill climb as it turns east toward Embudo Canyon. Along the way another popular mountain-biking route, Trail 401, branches to the south past the Embudo Trail parking area at the east end of Indian School Rd. Trail 401 roughly parallels the Foothills Trail, but is farther west, and can be followed to the Open Space area at the east end of Copper Blvd.

Trail 365 continues east to the boundary of the Sandia Mountain Wilderness and then turns south, crossing Embudo Trail (wp EMB365). The trail continues south, passing over a saddle point east of U-Mound about two miles later (wp EYEWP6). It drops through a couple of switchbacks and then continues to parallel the foothills toward the south. At the base of the switchbacks, an intersecting path leads east to the Copper Blvd. parking area (wp CUPARK).

The trail reaches another saddle point about 0.75 mile later (wp EYEWP1). From this saddle point, an alternate trail branches uphill and to the east leading to the "Eye of the Sandias" (described elsewhere). Continuing south, Trail 365 then begins to lose elevation sharply over the next quarter mile as it drops into a wide grassy valley just north of I-40. At the bottom of the hill, the trail swings west to reach its southern trailhead (wp 365STH) at Camino de la Sierra.

Length: 3.5 miles (one way)
Elevation: 6,450–8,810 feet
Rating: Difficult
See Map: 13 (page 100)

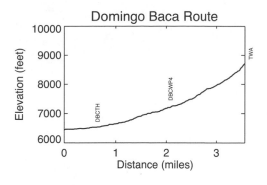

Domingo Baca Route

Driving Instructions: Take Tramway Boulevard north past Academy and turn east on Simms Park Road to the Elena Gallegos Picnic Area parking area. You must pay a parking fee at the guard shack on the way to the parking lot (wp 140TH): one dollar on weekdays, and two dollars on weekends.

Description

Warning: This is a remote and rugged area in the Sandia Mountains. The hike to the TWA crash site is not along an officially maintained trail. Do not attempt this hike by yourself, in case an emergency should arise. You should also be well prepared physically and have provisions to take care of yourself in the event of a mishap in the wilderness. I also recommend that you take a GPS, if you have one available, and use the waypoints that I have listed to help you find your way through this isolated area. (The 3.5 mile length listed above is the distance to the TWA crash site, and is not the distance to the junction with the upper segment of La Luz Trail.)

This hike goes high into Domingo Baca Canyon, a rugged part of the Sandia Mountains. The trail follows the main fork of Domingo Baca Canyon to the wreckage of a TWA flight that crashed on February 19, 1955, killing all sixteen people aboard. Thick cloud cover and a malfunctioning compass contributed to or caused the crash. The hike covers quite a range of terrain over its length. The lower part is bare and rocky, going up a sandy arroyo; the upper portion, which usually has flowing water, is lush and overgrown.

Follow several of the trails in the Elena Gallegos Picnic Area to the north for about a half mile making your way to the entrance to the Sandia Mountain Wilderness. There are signs along the way pointing to Domingo Baca Route. I recommend taking the first entrance into the

Fig. 16. Portion of the cockpit from the wreckage of TWA flight 260 in Domingo Baca Canyon.

wilderness (wp DBCTH) to avoid the many mountain bikers using the Open Space area. After a half-mile walk inside the wilderness area (wp DBCWP1), the trail begins to shift from its northeast direction, turning to the east.

The trail passes the ruins of an abandoned shelter (just its rock foundation remains) about a half-mile later (wp DBCWP2). The ruins are located about thirty feet north of the trail, at a spot where the main trail jogs south and crosses the streambed. The ruins make an interesting destination for hikers interested in a short hike, or families with children.

A key juncture in the hike to the TWA crash site is 0.2 miles east of the ruins just mentioned. You **must** be hiking in the streambed, within the thick tree cover, to find the key turnoff. Coming up to this spot, there is actually a better, well-worn trail to the north of the stream. You need to make your way down to the streambed itself. As you walk east along the streambed, look closely to your right (south) for a crude path taking you out of the streambed and up the twenty-foot-high embankment, toward the southeast. Two streambeds split at this spot; the left is usually dry and the right hand one often has flowing water and a dripping waterfall (a , couple of feet tall). The proper route goes to the right (east) at this junction (wp DBCWP3). Sometimes, a cairn marks the spot, but you cannot rely on it. If you miss this turnoff, staying left to continue up the streambed, you will soon run into a dead-end canyon blocked by a thirty-to-forty-foot-high wall of rocks. If you have a GPS, I recommend that you use the waypoint that I list (wp DBCWP3) to find the turn. The good news is that once you scramble up the embankment, there is a relatively well-worn trail for the following 1.6-mile hike up to the crash site. (However, the remainder of the trail is quite steep, gaining about fourteen hundred feet in elevation over that distance.)

The trail next crosses some open, sandy terrain for a short distance, and it then joins the streambed that it follows for the rest of the hike. After another 0.2 mile, the trail passes a nice area that is often used as a campsite (wp DBCWP4); I have heard that Boy Scouts sometime come up to this area for overnight camping trips.

The remaining hike up the rugged and steep canyon travels through dense tree cover. Along the way, you may hear the Sandia Peak Tramway passing overhead, but the trees are thick and you may not see it. When you are almost underneath the Tram wires, the trail veers to the north, heading directly toward the plane wreckage. The path becomes more rugged and less distinct as it makes its way up the slot canyon. There is a rock obstacle, about six feet high, that you have to scramble up along the way.

After about a quarter mile walk through the dense foliage, you should come upon the first pieces of the wreckage (wp TWA). On my last visit I saw a large piece of the fuselage with a red number 416 on the side and two rubber tires near the bottom of the wreckage site. As the trail continues up the canyon, there are hundreds of pieces of the plane strewn around, including identifiable parts of the engine, propellers, and landing gear. The site is humbling and rather sad to visit. I recommend that you treat it with respect, and think of the sixteen who died as you reach the area. Please do not remove any of the pieces from the area, no matter how small.

From here, you can continue hiking all of the way to the top of the mountain, intersecting La Luz Trail just below Kiwanis Cabin. However, the path virtually disappears at places along the way, and thick low-lying trees and brush block your progress if you lose the route. If you manage to follow the route it becomes quite steep, but no cliffs or exposure block your way.

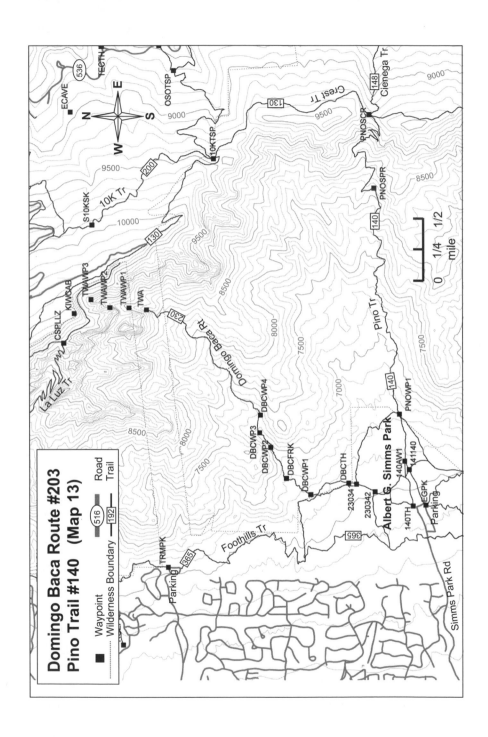

Domingo Baca Route #203
Pino Trail #140 (Map 13)

Waypoint
Wilderness Boundary

516 Road
192 Trail

Pino Trail (No. 140)

Length: 4.5 miles (one way)
Elevation: 6,460–9,230 feet
Rating: Moderate
See Map: 13 (page 100)
Driving Instructions: Take Tramway Boulevard north from Academy, then turn east on Simms Park Road leading to the Elena Gallegos Picnic Area (marked by signs). There is a fee to park (wp EGPK) that you must pay at the guard station, currently one dollar on weekdays and two dollars on weekends.

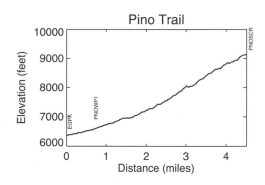

Description

Pino Trail offers a beautiful wilderness outing right at the edge of the city, and is one of the most popular trails in the Sandias. It was added to the trail system in 1988. The trail enters the Sandia Mountain Wilderness Area (wp PNOWP1) and goes east, up the south side of Pino Canyon. It travels to the ridgeline running between Sandia Crest and South Peak. Pino Trail is a scenic hike and a good workout. The lower portion can be hiked year round; the upper portion may be snow packed and icy from late fall to early spring.

The lower portion of the trail is dry and rocky, through sparse piñon-juniper cover. After about a mile, you get into more shade and tall tree cover. About three quarters way up the trail, you pass the tiny Pino Spring (wp PNOSPR). There are nice views of the rocky western face of the Sandias to the north along this stretch visible through breaks in the thick tree cover.

The upper portion of Pino Trail is a workout, both from the steeper grade and from the higher elevations. Pino Trail ends at its junction with the Crest Trail (wp PNOSCR). Take it slow and steady on the climb, and you will be rewarded with a beautiful vista from the ridgeline. A faint path leads to a roomy and impressive overlook at the top of the cliffs. The path to it is not obvious, however, and may require some searching out. (See the description of Cienega Trail for instructions on bushwhacking to the overlook.)

Extending your hike: The top of Pino Trail intersects the Crest Trail (wp PNOSCR), running north-south. You can explore some nice areas on a relatively flat trail by hiking in either direction along the Crest Trail as far as you like, then returning to hike down Pino Trail.

Cienega Trail comes up the mountain from the east side, and also meets Pino Trail and the Crest Trail at this spot. It is possible to take a nice "up and over" hike, by leaving a car at the Cienega trailhead, and hiking up the west side of the Sandias on Pino Trail, then down the eastern slope on Cienega Trail.

Embudito Trail (No. 192)

Length: 6 miles (one way)
Elevation: 6,240–9,400 feet
Rating: Difficult
See Map: 14 (page 103)
Driving Instructions: Take Montgomery Blvd. east from Tramway to Glenwood Hills Dr., and turn left. Follow Glenwood Hills north for one-third

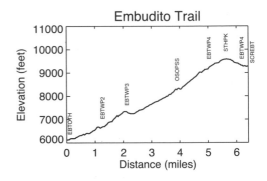

mile and you will see a sign pointing to Embudito Trail on your right. Turn on Trailhead Rd., and it leads you to the parking area (wp EBTOTH).

Description

Embudito Trail is a popular and well-traveled trail. However, the farther up you go, the less likely you will run into other hikers. It is the route that I most often take to reach South Peak. *Embudito* is Spanish for "little funnel," describing the tight canyon that leads to Oso Pass.

The bottom section of Embudito Trail has been rerouted north of the sandy arroyo that it used to follow. The trail now initially heads north and scales the south-facing slope of the canyon. The trail follows this slope around to the east and passes through a small plateau, about a hundred feet above the stream (wp EBTPLT), where the path seems to split into

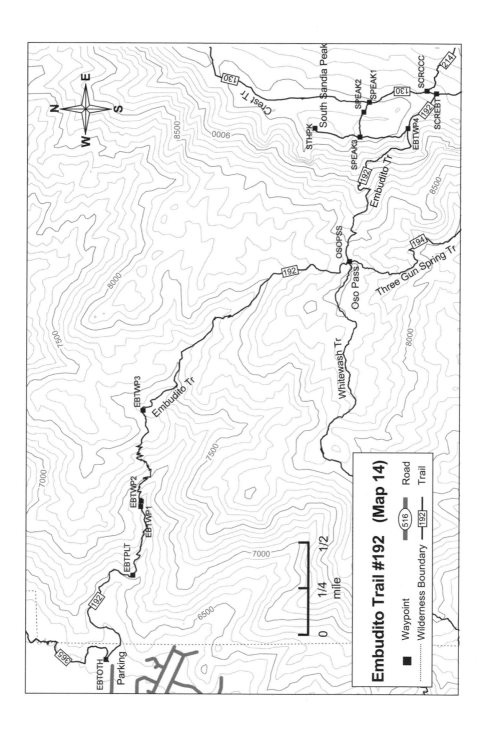

Embudito Trail #192 (Map 14)

■ Waypoint

········ Wilderness Boundary

──〈516〉── Road

──〈192〉── Trail

several different branches. Looking toward the south, one or two paths go over the rise, and you will see that they start heading down toward the canyon bottom. You want to take the branch just to the left of those paths and head uphill past a large boulder. It is easy to take the wrong fork here, because the paths appear almost equally worn. (Casual hikers often go no farther than here.)

The next portion of Embudito Trail is rocky, sparsely vegetated, and steep in places. About a mile and a half into the hike, the trail takes a dip to the streambed (wp EBTWP1). However, after only fifty yards there should be a gray signpost (wp EBTWP2) pointing the way to the left and back out of the streambed.

After another three-quarters of a mile or so, the trail returns to the canyon bottom. The route gets into more tree cover and shade, and becomes increasingly pleasant. Embudito Trail then crosses the streambed and switches to the north-facing slope of the canyon, which is lush and green. I think this is one of the most beautiful areas in the Sandia Mountains.

Four miles into the hike you reach Oso Pass (wp OSOPSS). From Oso Pass, Embudito Trail continues eastward toward the main ridgeline and South Sandia Peak. This next section of trail is steep and relentless, especially after you have already hiked for a couple hours.

You will reach a turnoff (wp EBTWP4) to South Peak from Embudito Trail about a mile past Oso Pass shortly before you reach the main north-south ridgeline. Look carefully to your left to spot a small secondary trail leading uphill; this trail heads in a northwest direction from Embudito Trail, then eventually turns straight uphill. There is usually a cairn marking this turnoff.

If you want the shortest route to South Peak, take this turn and head up. South Peak is about 0.6 mile north of this point. The unmaintained trail is steep for the first 0.1 mile. After passing through some Gambel oak thickets, the trail enters a meadow west of the ridgeline. It then climbs steeply onto the final summit ridge. The last thirty yards to South Peak involve scrambling up a steep path with loose gravel. The 360° views from South Peak are spectacular, and are a fitting reward after a long hike. (See the section entitled "South Sandia Peak" for more discussion of the area and a detailed map.)

Retrace your steps down from South Peak to Embudito Trail (wp EBTWP4), or use the following alternate route down to visit the beautiful meadows of South Peak. Hike south 0.25 mile from the peak on the same route that you came up, to a clearing at 9,600' elevation (wp SPEAK3). From here, you should head east (to your left) over the ridgeline and some low, craggy rocks toward the Crest Trail. You will probably see a cairn or two marking the way (wp SPEAK2), and you will join the Crest Trail (wp SPEAK1) about 0.4 mile north of its junction with Embudito Trail. The broad grassy meadows are one of the highlights of the Sandia Mountains, and I love the area. Follow the Crest Trail south to its intersection with Embudito Trail (wp SCREBT). Turn right onto Embudito Trail and proceed over Deer Pass and then down the mountain to return home.

Embudo Trail (No. 193)

Length: 3.2 miles (one way)
Elevation: 6,180–7,860 feet
Rating: Moderate
See Map: 15 (page 106)
Driving Instructions: From Tramway Blvd., go east on Indian School Road until it ends at the large paved parking area for Embudo Trail (wp INSCPK).

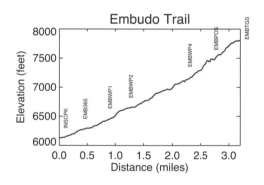

Description

Embudo Trail is a popular hiking destination on the lower west side of the mountain. The trail travels east through Embudo Canyon. Embudo Trail is a nice, moderate day hike. It can also be used as part of a much more rigorous route to South Sandia Peak.

Embudo Trail heads east from the parking area, passing a large water tank and flood-control dam. The trail enters the Sandia Mountain Wilderness at its intersection with the Foothills Trail No. 365 (wp EMB365). The sandy Embudo Trail continues east to the entrance of a tight canyon opening (wp EMBWP1). *Embudo* is Spanish for "funnel," in

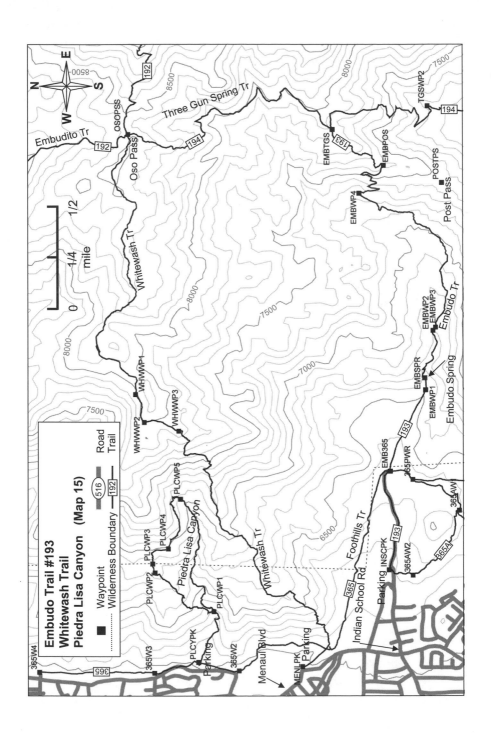

Embudo Trail #193
Whitewash Trail
Piedra Lisa Canyon (Map 15)

Waypoint
·········· Wilderness Boundary

516 Road
192 Trail

reference to this tight canyon, which drains the broader expanse to the east. It is easy to lose the trail through this stretch. However, as you go through this narrow canyon, you never need to go to the south side of the stream; if you keep looking to your left (and up) as you make your way, a trail will be there. In wet years, Embudo Spring feeds a waterfall over an eight-foot-tall masonry wall about 150 feet into the canyon (wp EMBSPR). Many casual hikers will go no farther than this spring, which is a short but easy and worthwhile destination.

After you get through the tight rocky area, begin walking up the sandy canyon bottom, which will soon split into a "Y" (wp EMBWP2). Take the south (right) branch at this "Y." After only one hundred feet or so, look for an opportunity to walk up a small ten-foot embankment (wp EMBWP3). On top of the embankment, Embudo Trail is well worn and hard packed. (Heads up! If you miss this little juncture, you will no longer be on Embudo Trail. I've been there; done that . . .)

The pleasant hike up Embudo Trail makes its way to the east end of the Embudo Canyon bowl. It is about a mile hike through the generally flat, dry, and brushy canyon bottom. The trail then begins a series of switchbacks (wp EMBWP4) that take you to the upper portion of the canyon. At the top of the switchbacks, you come upon a saddle point (wp EMBPOS), which turns off to Post Pass to the south. The path to Post Pass is usually blocked with a line of small rocks to keep the casual hiker from making the wrong turn. You should take the left turn and continue up Embudo Trail.

It is about another one third of a mile along Embudo Trail to reach the intersection with Three Gun Spring Trail (wp EMBTGS). This is a steep portion of the trail, so be prepared for a little workout. Embudo Trail ends at its junction with Three Gun Spring Trail.

Extending your hike: From the junction just mentioned (wp EMBTGS), it is an enjoyable walk north to Oso Pass (wp OSOPSS) along Three Gun Spring Trail, which is about a mile and a half away. From Oso Pass you have several more options, including a 1.5-mile hike up to South Sandia Peak along Embudito Trail, or north for four miles to the Embudito Trailhead. Whitewash Trail heads west from Oso Pass and exits the mountain just north of the Embudo parking area. The route of Embudo Trail to Oso Pass and back on Whitewash Trail makes a scenic ten-mile loop hike that I enjoy.

Three Gun Spring Trail (No. 194)

Length: 4 miles (one way)
Elevation: 6,320–8,460 feet
Rating: Moderate
See Map: 16 (page 110)
Driving Instructions: Drive east from Albuquerque on I-40, take the Carnuel exit, and go 1.5 miles east on old Route 66. There is a brown hiking sign marking the turnoff from Route 66 into the Monticello subdivision, providing access to the trail.

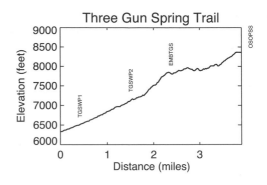

Follow residential streets to the trailhead. Park in the dirt lot at the trailhead, marked by signs (wp TGSTH). This parking area is sometimes plagued by vandalism, so don't leave valuables within view inside your parked car.

Description

Three Gun Spring Trail is a great hike, with panoramic views of Tijeras Canyon and I-40 to the south, and Albuquerque across Embudo Canyon to the west. It is an ideal trail to take in the winter; the direct sunshine and lack of shade on the lower portion of the trail can make it a hot hike in summer months. It is legend that three Spanish conquistador pistols were found in the area, which gives rise to the name of the canyon and spring. Decades ago a wooden water trough near the spring was also carved with the image of three pistols, but the trough has long since disappeared.

From the parking area, it is about a half mile walk north to reach the entry to the Sandia Mountain Wilderness (wp TGSWP1). There is a large Forest Service sign at this spot with a map of all the trails in the Sandia Mountains. Continuing north, about three-quarters of a mile past the sign, at the foot of the first set of switchbacks at the north end of the canyon, there is a turnoff to the east toward Three Gun Spring itself (wp TGSWP2). However, you should stay to the left to continue up the main trail.

The series of switchbacks going up the south-facing slope of the canyon makes for a good workout. The steep, rocky terrain is exposed to the sun, with no shade to speak of. This portion is especially steep during the last third of a mile, or so. The trail makes an eighteen-hundred-foot elevation gain in the two-mile hike from the parking area to the top of the switchbacks.

At the top of the canyon is the intersection of Three Gun Spring Trail with Embudo Trail, marked by a signpost (wp EMBTGS). Embudo Trail comes up from Embudo Canyon to the west. Three Gun Spring Trail continues to the north around the upper portion of Embudo Canyon and terminates at Oso Pass. In contrast to the lower section of this trail, the hike to Oso Pass is lush, tree covered, and cool. This portion of the hike is about a mile and a half, and crosses a couple of small streams along the way.

Oso Pass (wp OSOPSS) is a significant spot, with trails converging from four directions. Three Gun Spring Trail arrives at Oso Pass from the south, and Whitewash Trail comes in from the west. Embudito Trail reaches this point from the north, and continues to the east, heading up to Deer Pass and South Sandia Peak.

Fig. 17. Distinctive rock formation along Three Gun Spring Trail.

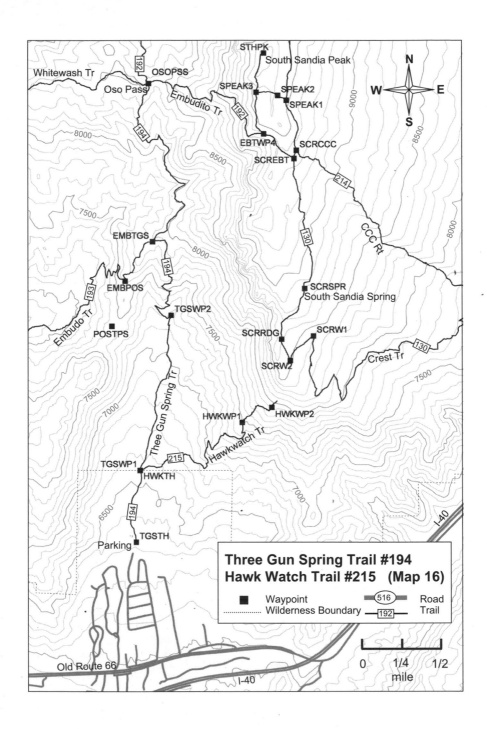

Three Gun Spring Trail #194
Hawk Watch Trail #215   (Map 16)

■ Waypoint	⬭516⬭	Road
⋯⋯⋯⋯ Wilderness Boundary	192	Trail

STHPK
South Sandia Peak
Whitewash Tr
192
OSOPSS
Oso Pass
SPEAK3
SPEAK2
SPEAK1
Embudito Tr
192
194
8000
8500
EBTWP4
SCRCCC
SCREBT
214
CCC Rt
130
8000
7500
EMBTGS
8000
194
EMBPOS
193
SCRSPR
South Sandia Spring
Embudo Tr
TGSWP2
POSTPS
7500
SCRRDG
SCRW1
SCRW2
Crest Tr
130
7500
7500
7000
Thee Gun Spring Tr
HWKWP1
HWKWP2
Hawkwatch Tr
TGSWP1
215
7000
HWKTH
6500
194
I-40
TGSTH
Parking
Old Route 66
I-40

Extending your hike: Hike up Three Gun Spring Trail to Oso Pass and then continue east on Embudito Trail for a good route to South Sandia Peak. Or, if you leave a second car at the Embudito Trail parking area, you have the alternative to continue north from Oso Pass for a four-mile hike along Embudito Trail rather than retracing your steps on Three Gun Spring Trail.

Hawk Watch Trail (No. 215)

Length: 2 miles (one way)
Elevation: 6,300–7,900 feet
Rating: Moderate
See Map: 16 (page 110)
Driving Instructions: Drive east from Albuquerque on I-40, take the Carnuel exit, and go 1.5 miles east on old Route 66. There is a brown hiking sign marking the turnoff from Route 66 into

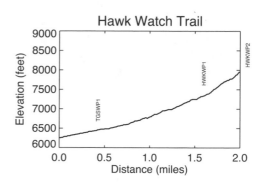

the Monticello subdivision, providing access to the trail. Follow residential streets to the Three Gun Spring Trail parking area (wp TGSTH). This parking area is sometimes plagued by vandalism, so don't leave valuables within view inside your parked car.

Description

Hawk Watch Trail is an offshoot from Three Gun Spring Trail. The trail is named after Hawk Watch International, an organization that studies raptors (hawks, eagles, and other birds of prey) by counting birds in their flyways and by trapping and banding birds at different locations around the world. Hawk Watch Trail was constructed to accommodate their activities. The raptor banding operation is conducted from February 22 through May 5 every year. The peak in the migration season is around the last week in March and the first week in April. Visitors are welcome to observe the birds and trapping and banding activities. Volunteers at the site will be glad to explain their activities (I hear that they appreciate

Fig. 18. Sign pointing to the observation area of Hawk Watch Trail.

chocolate; the volunteers, that is, not the hawks.) Call the Albuquerque Field Office at 255–7622 for more information.

The hike begins along Three Gun Spring Trail and follows it for about a half mile to the entrance of the Sandia Mountain Wilderness (wp TGSWP1). Immediately north of this entrance, there is a sign for Hawk Watch Trail, which heads to the east. Hawk Watch Trail is steep, but easy to follow. There are great views into Three Gun Spring Canyon, and south to I-40 and Tijeras Canyon. After about a mile and a quarter, Hawk Watch Trail reaches a flat ridge (wp HWKWP1), about seventy-four hundred feet in elevation. The bird counters with Hawk Watch International conduct their surveys from the rocky area at the south end of this plateau. Hawk Watch Trail officially ends at this point.

The hike down is quite steep in places and the footing can be uncertain because of the loose, sandy gravel on the trail. Be careful on your way back down the slope.

Extending your hike: (Please do not take the additional hike described below during Hawk Watch International's observation season. Doing so would disturb their sensitive studies.) There is a less-distinct, steep trail continuing up the slope toward the east that you can follow for about a half mile from the turnaround point described above (wp HWKWP1). In the steepest places traction can be a problem on this stretch. The trail works its way to the east (and upward). At an elevation of about seventy-nine hundred feet, the trail reaches another one of the Hawk Watch International study sites (wp HWKWP2).

More adventurous hikers can continue farther up, even as far as the Crest Trail. This route joins the Crest Trail at a beautiful overlook above Tijeras Canyon. From there, you may continue up the Crest Trail for 1.25 miles to the junction with Embudito Trail (wp SCREBT), then west on Embudito Trail for 1.25 miles to Oso Pass (wp OSOPSS), and finally south on Three Gun Spring Trail for 4 miles to your car. This 9.3 mile loop has a total elevation gain of nearly 3,200 feet and is a wonderful day's hike.

CCC Route (No. 214)

Length: 1.8 miles (one way)
Elevation: 7,580–9,345 feet
Rating: Difficult
See Map: 17 (page 114)
Driving Instructions: The CCC Route is accessed from the south end of the Crest Trail. Travel east on I-40 from Albuquerque, then take the south Tijeras exit. After the exit, turn left to go under

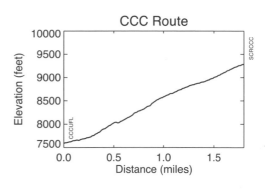

the highway, and then turn right to Canyon Estates. Follow the residential road to the trailhead parking lot (wp SCRSPK).

Description
CCC Route is a steep hike, gaining over 1,750 feet in elevation along its 1.8-mile length. The route is named for the Civilian Conservation Corps, who constructed the trail in the 1930s (along with many other projects around the Sandia Mountains). It provides a short, direct route to or from the South Peak area.

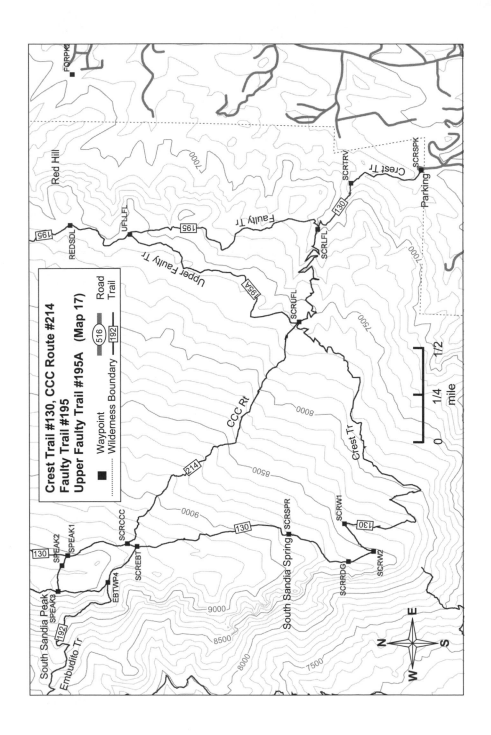

Crest Trail #130, CCC Route #214
Faulty Trail #195
Upper Faulty Trail #195A (Map 17)

Waypoint
Wilderness Boundary
516 Road
192 Trail

I usually combine the CCC Route with the Crest Trail, hiking up one and down the other to make a loop. I prefer to walk up the more modest grade of the Crest Trail, and then down the steeper CCC Route. Hiking up CCC Route leaves me panting for air and stopping every few hundred yards to rest. However, since going downhill is hard on many people's knees, you might prefer taking the loop in the reverse direction. Either way, the CCC Route is a great challenge for more advanced hikers.

To reach the lower trailhead for the CCC Route, hike up the Crest Trail for about two miles to the intersection with Upper Faulty Trail (wp SCRUFL). About fifty yards north of this junction, CCC Route heads northwest through a clearing (wp CCCUFL). There is usually a large pile of rocks (cairn) marking the trailhead.

The upper trailhead for the CCC Route is about one hundred yards north of the junction of the Crest Trail and Embudito Trail. This spot is six miles up the Crest Trail from the Canyon Estates trailhead.

The upper trailhead for CCC Route is a little tricky to locate. It is not marked by a sign because it is not part of the official Forest Service trail system (hence the designator "Route" in its name, rather than "Trail"). From the Embudito signpost (wp SCREBT), go north on the Crest Trail for about one hundred yards, and look for a couple of faint paths heading over a small ridge toward the east. This tops the CCC Route (wp SCRCCC). Once you are on top of the little ridge, you will probably see some small cairns which reassure that you've found the trail.

CCC Route is indistinct in many places; pay close attention as you hike. Fortunately, there are usually many cairns along the route marking the way. From the lower trailhead the path travels northwest along a ridge straight up the mountain. Switchbacks to cut the elevation grade are not to be found here. The lower portion of the trail travels through thick piñon and ponderosa pine, obscuring any long views of the surroundings. The upper portion of CCC Route passes through Gambel oak, and the trail is more open in many places, providing views to the south and east. However, with these openings comes direct exposure to the sun and rocky ground. This makes for some hot hiking near the top of the trail during the summer months.

Extending your hike: As mentioned before, a loop can be made by combining the Crest Trail and CCC Route. It is less than a mile to South Sandia Peak from the upper trailhead of CCC Route. Hiking routes to the peak are described separately in the section titled "South Sandia Peak."

Another loop can be made by hiking up Bart's Trail or Cañoncito Trail, south on the Crest Trail to visit South Peak, then down CCC Route, and north on Faulty Trail to close the loop. This loop is over twelve miles, but it makes a beautiful day's outing in the scenic southern end of the mountain.

Cañoncito Trail (No. 150)

Length: 3 miles (one way)
Elevation: 7,310–9,210 feet
Rating: Moderate
See Map: 18 (page 118)
Driving Instructions: The turnoff to Cañoncito trailhead is 3.4 miles north of I-40 on NM 14. Turn west on Cañoncito street from NM 14. Follow the main paved road for 0.4 mile until the pavement ends at a fork in the road. Take the left fork for 0.2 mile and park outside the locked metal gate (wp CNCPK).

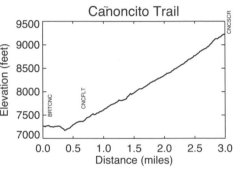

The road beyond the gate is private property for the next 0.8 mile. In the spring of 2001, the dirt road was closed to public vehicle access. Hikers wishing access to Cañoncito/Bart's Trail can park to the side of the road outside the gate. (Please be sure not to block any private driveways or traffic when you park.) The private landowners currently allow hikers to walk up the road to the trailhead. Please respect their private property. The locked gate adds about one extra mile on foot at the beginning and at the end of your hike.

Description

From the parking area outside the locked metal gate (wp CNCPK), walk up the road to the trailhead proper (wp BRTCNC), which is about one mile from your car. Cañoncito Trail and Bart's Trail begin from the same spot and are each marked by Forest Service signs. *Cañoncito* is Spanish for "little canyon," named for the tight canyon that the trail enters about one-half mile from the trailhead.

The first portion of Cañoncito Trail makes an arc from northeast to northwest contouring its way toward Faulty Trail. The route goes through thick piñon-juniper cover and occasional cactus along the way. After 0.4 mile the trail passes the ruins of an old stone building on the right side of the trail. You will come upon a beautiful series of about a dozen waterfalls, one to four feet high, 0.7 mile from the trailhead (wp CNCTRV). The falls were created from a travertine rock formation, a light-colored porous calcite ($CaCO_3$) material deposited from solution in ground or surface waters that contain lime. Usually there is a beautiful flowing stream coming down a twenty-foot embankment just up the hill from the travertine formations. Cañoncito Spring is marked by a sign on the left side of the trail about fifty yards before the junction with Faulty Trail (wp CNCFLT), 0.75 mile into the hike.

Cañoncito Trail enters the Sandia Mountain Wilderness west of Faulty Trail. The next portion of the trail becomes rocky and steep as it heads up the mountain. About a mile past Faulty Trail, 8,300' elevation, the surface of the trail becomes soft soil and the trail cuts a narrower path through spruce-fir coverage. In places the trail is deep and eroded as it passes through grassy clearings. This portion of the trail abounds with wildflowers in late spring and summer.

A quarter mile before reaching the main mountain ridgeline, the trail turns rocky through oak and aspen tree coverage. Cañoncito Trail terminates at its junction with the Crest Trail at about 9,200' elevation, three miles into the trail (wp CNCSCR). The tree coverage at the trail's end is rather thick. However, there are great views to the west a short distance south of this spot along the Crest Trail.

Extending your hike: A rewarding hiking route to South Sandia Peak continues south along the Crest Trail for about two miles (to wp SPEAK1) and then west across an open meadow to the ridge line and finally back north to South Peak. (See the section titled "South Sandia Peak" for more details.)

From the junction of Cañoncito Trail and the Crest Trail, it is only 0.75 mile south on the Crest Trail to the upper trailhead of Bart's Trail, marked by a sign (wp BRTSCR). You can take Bart's Trail down the mountain creating a satisfying loop hike. Note that the hike down Bart's Trail is quite steep, so hikers with bad knees might not enjoy this route home.

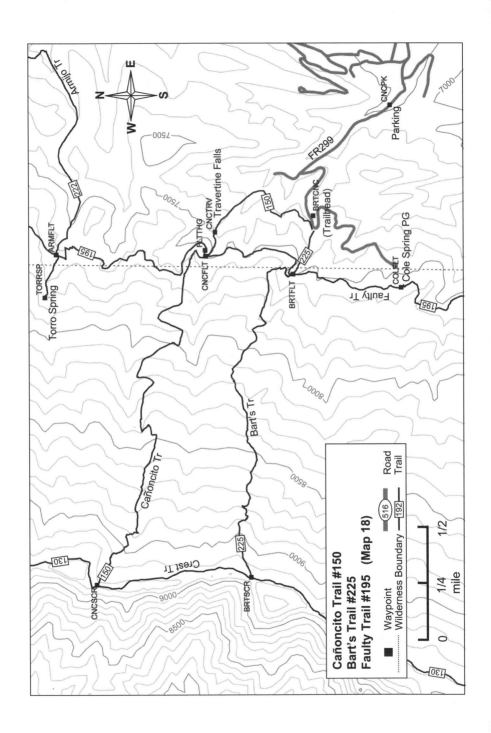

Cañoncito Trail #150
Bart's Trail #225
Faulty Trail #195   (Map 18)

■ Waypoint   ▬▬▬ 516 Road
⋯⋯⋯ Wilderness Boundary   ▬▬▬ 192 Trail

0   1/4   1/2
        mile

Length: 2 miles (one way)
Elevation: 7,300–9,140 feet
Rating: Moderate
See Map: 18 (page 118)
Driving Instructions: The turnoff to Bart's trailhead is 3.4 miles north of I-40 on NM 14. Turn west on Cañoncito street from NM 14. Follow the main paved road for 0.4 mile until the pavement ends at a fork in the road.

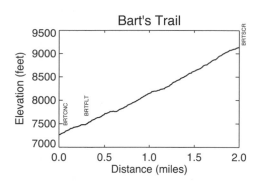

Take the left fork for 0.2 mile and park outside the locked metal gate (wp CNCPK). The road beyond the gate is private property for the next 0.8 mile. In the spring of 2001, the dirt road was closed to public-vehicle access. Hikers wishing access to Cañoncito / Bart's Trail can park to the side of the road outside the gate. (Please be sure not to block any private driveways or traffic when you park.) The private landowners currently allow hikers to walk up the road to the trailhead. Please respect their private property. The locked gate adds about one extra mile on foot at the beginning and at the end of your hike.

Description

Bart's Trail is a short, but steep, route to the main Sandia Mountain ridge-line from the east. It provides the quickest access to the beautiful South Sandia Peak area. Bart's Trail is named for Fayette "Bart" Barton, a long beloved Sandia Mountain hiking enthusiast. Bart constructed the original trail with assistance from friends in the New Mexico Mountain Club. The trail was eventually rerouted in places and incorporated into the official Forest Service trail system.

Cañoncito Trail and Bart's Trail share a common trailhead (wp BRTCNC) alongside the Forest Service road to Cole Spring Picnic Ground (FR 299). Bart's Trail heads west from the trailhead along the canyon bottom. After 0.1 mile the trail lifts out of the canyon bottom, and it begins a steep climb toward Faulty Trail, which it meets 0.1 mile later (wp BRTFLT). Bart's Trail then gets down to the serious business of climbing the mountain. The remainder of the two-mile trail continues a steep uphill grade with few switchbacks or concessions to the faint of heart (or lungs or knees). It is quite a workout, but nonetheless, it is a trail that I enjoy.

The lower section of the trail travels through piñon-juniper forest, with cactus and yucca plants alongside the path. This section of the trail is rocky and can be hard on your feet. Around eighty-three hundred feet in elevation—a little over a mile into the trail—the path travels over softer ground. Thick grass lines the trail through small clearings. Wildflowers also decorate some of these clearings in spring and summer.

The trail continues west on its relentless and steep grade toward the ridgeline. About 1.8 miles into the hike, Bart's Trail passes through a broad, rocky clearing. Although this is a sure sign that you are near the end of the uphill climb, this section is hot and exposed to the sun. The final two hundred yards pass through thick oak cover before reaching the Crest Trail at an elevation of 9,140 feet (wp BRTSCR).

Extending your hike: It is about a 1.5 mile hike south on the Crest Trail to reach South Sandia Peak. The trail follows relatively flat terrain and is easy to hike. Beautiful views to the east and the west open up along the way. Broad open meadows below South Peak make this area one of the most scenic in the Sandia Mountains. (See the section titled "South Sandia Peak" for more information about the area.)

The upper trailhead for Cañoncito Trail is 0.75 mile north of Bart's Trail along the Crest Trail (wp BRTCNC). Hiking down Cañoncito Trail makes for a nice loop hike. In addition, Cañoncito Trail is much less steep than Bart's, and some hikers will prefer its gentler slope down the mountain.

Other Hiking Routes

North Mystery Trail

Length: 5.2 miles (one way)
Elevation: 7,360–8,110 feet
Rating: Moderate
See Map: 19 (page 124)

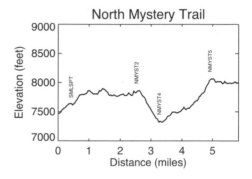

Driving Instructions: I recommend taking two cars for this hike. To find the trailhead and starting point for the hike, take I-40 east from Albuquerque, then go north on NM 14 for six miles, and take the turnoff to the Crest Highway (NM 536). Drive 2.4 miles along the Crest Highway, and park on the left side of the road at a long pullout (wp NMYPRK) just before a sharp turn in the road. (The pullout is 0.4 miles past the turnoff to the Doc Long Picnic Ground.). Leave a second car waiting for you at the parking area for the Palomas Cliffs Trail, where you will finish the hike. To find that parking area, continue up the Crest Highway for 4.9 miles to the turnoff at the Balsam Glade Picnic Area. Take NM 165W north, down Capulin Canyon for 2.1 miles to a small parking area on the right (north) side at a bend in the road (wp PLPKTH).

Description

Several hiking trails in the Sandia Mountains were created unofficially by individuals or groups and later they were incorporated into the system of trails recognized by the Forest Service. Two notable examples are Bart's

Trail and the Faulty Trail. The trail now recognized as Faulty Trail was created by unknown persons in 1975 (south of Cañoncito Trail) and then extended in pieces to the north through the 1980s. The original route was called the Diamond Trail by some people, for the distinctive diamond blazes cut into tree trunks marking the way. It was also called Mystery Trail by others because of its unknown creator.

In a similar circumstance, a trail of unknown origin has been forged north from Barro Canyon to Lagunita Seca (below Palomas Peak). The trail is blazed with diamond cuts into tree trunks along the route. This trail actually begins at the intersection of Sulphur Canyon Trail and the Faulty Trail (wp FLTSUL) and runs northeast for two miles across the Crest Highway at the bend in the road described above (wp NMYPRK). I have designated this unnamed trail from Sulphur Canyon to Lagunita Seca the North Mystery Trail in keeping with its predecessor. It is possible that one day the trail will be adopted by the Forest Service. In fact it could arguably be designated a continuation of the Faulty Trail. Time will tell.

The trail passes through a beautiful area of the mountain that is not intersected by other established hiking routes. I have suggested beginning the hike at the Crest Highway for ease of access, rather than at the southern starting point in Sulphur Canyon.

North Mystery Trail heads up Barro Canyon north of the Crest Highway from the hairpin turn. (*Barro* is Spanish for "clay.") The first portion of the trail keeps to the eastern slope just above the canyon bottom. After 0.4 miles the trail comes to a distinct saddle point (wp SMLSPT). North Mystery Trail goes west, up the hill from the saddle point; look for diamond blazes on the trees.

Another short trail, called Smelter Trail, goes down the wash and north from this saddle point. It heads toward the ruins of an old smelter, from which the trail gets its name. Smelter Trail continues north about one mile, and ends at a fence (wp SMLEND) marked with No Trespassing and Private Property signs. The smelter ruins are just beyond the fence on the private property and are not available for visiting.

North Mystery Trail climbs steeply uphill from the saddle point to the top of a canyon (wp NMYST1). The trail continues north on relatively flat terrain for almost two miles through beautiful and isolated country. There are nice views of Tecolote Peak to the west through this stretch. North Mystery Trail passes through a noticeable saddle point 2.3 miles into the hike (wp NMYST2) at elevation 7,960', then begins a steep dip into Madera Canyon. The trail passes under a set of power lines at 2.7 miles (wp NMYST3); look to the west for impressive views of Capulin Peak and Madera Canyon. The trail reaches the lush canyon bottom 0.3 miles later (wp NMYST4), elevation 7,360'. A streambed and old logging road cross the trail at the canyon bottom. *Madera* is Spanish for "wood" or "lumber."

North Mystery Trail continues north, out of the canyon through a steep uphill section. Palomas Peak comes into view ahead when you have neared the top of your climb. North Mystery Trail ends at the southeast edge of the beautiful meadow of Lagunita Seca (wp NMYST5), elevation 8,110', which is 4.4 miles into the hike. The trail enters the meadow just south of a tall ponderosa pine that has large diamond blazes on its south and north sides. *Lagunita seca* is Spanish for the "small, dry lake" from which this meadow was formed.

If you have left a second car at the Palomas Cliffs parking area, continue west across the meadow through some openings in the trees to meet a worn trail (wp NMYST6). This is the Palomas Cliffs Trail, described next in this book. Go left on this trail to make your way to your second car, about 0.7 mile.

Extending your hike: From the west end of Lagunita Seca you can extend your hike by following the Palomas Cliffs Trail to the right, and up the slope (from wp NMYST6). See the Palomas Cliffs Trail discussion for more details.

You may also extend your outing by retracing your path for the 4.4 miles along North Mystery Trail from Lagunita Seca back to the Crest Highway. This option makes an enjoyable nine-mile hike (and also simplifies the logistics of dropping off a second car at the north end.)

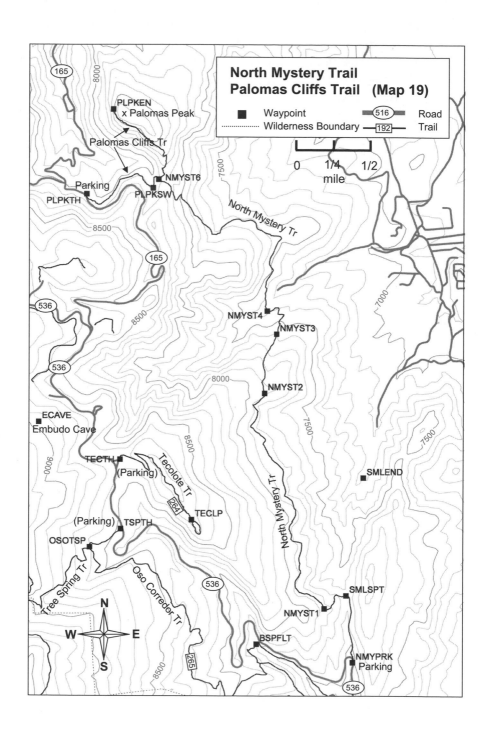

North Mystery Trail
Palomas Cliffs Trail (Map 19)

■ Waypoint   ⬭516⬭ Road
.... Wilderness Boundary   —[192]— Trail

0   1/4   1/2
mile

⟮165⟯

8000

PLPKEN
x Palomas Peak

Palomas Cliffs Tr

7500

Parking   ■ NMYST6
PLPKTH   PLPKSW

North Mystery Tr

8500

⟮165⟯

⟮536⟯

8500

NMYST4 ■   ■ NMYST3

7000

8000

■ NMYST2

7500

■ ECAVE
Embudo Cave

9000

TECTH ■
(Parking)   Tecolote Tr

8500

7500   7500

264   ■ SMLEND

■ TECLP

(Parking) ■ TSPTH

OSOTSP ■

North Mystery Tr

Tree Spring Tr   Oso Corredor Tr

⟮536⟯

■ SMLSPT

NMYST1 ■

N
W   E
S

265

8500

■ BSPFLT

■ NMYPRK
Parking

⟮536⟯

Palomas Cliffs Trail

Length: 1.5 miles (one way)
Elevation: 8,010–8,560 feet
Rating: Moderate
See Map: 3 (page 40);
19 (page 124)
Driving Instructions: To find the Palomas Cliffs trailhead, drive east from Albuquerque on I-40 to the Tijeras exit, then north on NM 14 about six miles to the Crest Highway (NM 536). Drive 7.3 miles up the Crest

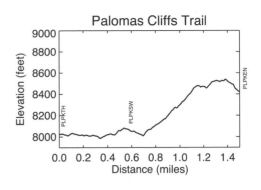

Highway to the turnoff at the Balsam Glade Picnic Area. Take NM 165W north toward Placitas. This is a bumpy, dusty dirt road, but it should be passable for most passenger vehicles. Travel 2.1 miles down NM 165W to a small parking area on the right (north) side at a bend in the road (wp PLPKTH). The parking area is just after you pass a slope to your left that was burned in a 1990 fire. There are no signs at this parking area, but there are three concrete barriers to look for. (If you see the sign for the Sandia Conference Center on the left side of the road, you have gone 0.3 miles too far.) NM 165W may be snow packed and icy from about November to April each year. However, if the gate is open, you are allowed to drive through.

Description

Palomas Cliffs Trail, an unofficial hiking trail in the Capulin Canyon / Las Huertas Canyon area, is primarily used by rock climbers for access to the limestone cliffs of Palomas Peak. *Palomas* is Spanish for "doves," but the usage here may refer to band-tail pigeons alluding to the limestone bands across the peak.

To find the beginning of the trail, walk uphill along the road (roughly southeast) for about seventy-five feet, then look down and to your left. A well-established trail that parallels the dirt road heads east from this point. It is well worth making sure that you are on the right path. A common mistake is to go north down the slope from the parking area to the bottom of the deep valley.

After about a half mile (wp PLPKSW), the trail crosses a streambed at a sharp switchback. Shortly afterward, the trail passes the entrance to Lagunita Seca meadow (wp NMYST6), marked on most maps. The meadow is a beautiful spot to spend some time and have a picnic lunch. However, the Palomas Cliffs Trail itself goes left from the entrance to the meadow and continues uphill.

The trail makes its way toward, but not all the way to, Palomas Peak, overlooking Las Huertas Canyon. The trail ends up following the limestone cliffs that run below the peak. The trail ends as it wraps around to the west side of the peak (wp PLPKEN), overlooking Las Huertas Picnic Area on the road far below.

North Sandia Peak

Length: 1.8 miles (one way)
Elevation: 10,200–10,600 feet
Rating: Moderate
See Map: 20 (page 128)
Driving Instructions: Go east on I-40 from Albuquerque, north on NM 14 for 6 miles, drive up the Crest Highway (NM 536) for 13.4 miles to the top of the mountain, and park at the main parking lot (wp CRSTPK).

Description
North Sandia Peak, a significant landmark in the Sandia Mountains, stands two miles north of Sandia Crest. The huge granite face of the Shield on the mountain's western face is instantly recognizable to all who live in the area. North Sandia Peak is the green summit above the Shield.

Begin this hike on the Crest Trail, walking north from the Crest trailhead, which is east of the radio towers and marked by a large Forest Service sign. The first portion of the Crest Trail runs next to a chain-link fence, then passes through a meadow at 0.35 mile. Immediately afterward the trail enters the Sandia Mountain Wilderness. One half mile into the hike you pass a sign that says "Del Agua Overlook 1.5 miles" (wp CHMTH). (A faint trail heading west from this point, then turning sharply south, is the beginning of the Chimney Canyon Route). There is

Fig. 19. View of North Sandia Peak from Del Agua Overlook.

an impressive overlook about two hundred yards north of here along the Crest Trail, where you can view the Shield and North Sandia Peak above it. The large rock formation to the south of the Shield is the Needle, another prominent landmark.

About 0.9 mile into the hike (wp NPKOL1) a faint trail branches off to the west to a beautiful overlook along the ridgeline. You can walk along the bare, broken shale edge of the ridgeline for about a tenth of a mile with spectacular views of the Shield, Needle, and the precipitous canyon below. Please be very cautious to keep away from the sharp falloff from the edge. When you reach the north end of the bare ridgeline, you can see a faint trail heading to the east and then north. This path will take you back to the main Crest Trail (wp NPKOL2).

The Crest Trail drops below the ridgeline 0.1 mile after you return to the Crest Trail from the overlook. The Crest Trail swings about one hundred feet east of the ridge for 0.1 mile and then climbs toward the ridge once again (wp NPKWP1). As the trail moves up to the ridge, look for a faint path branching off to the west and heading toward the ridgeline (the Crest Trail will stay below the ridge here).

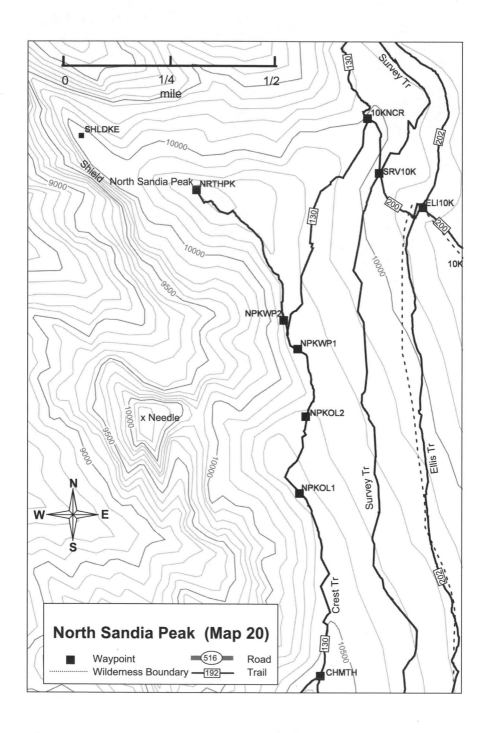

North Sandia Peak (Map 20)

■ Waypoint   ⬤516⬤ Road
···· Wilderness Boundary —[192]— Trail

The branch to the west will take you to North Sandia Peak, traveling north and then west. This unmaintained route is indistinct in some places. However, it typically hugs the ridgeline within twenty feet or so. If you lose the trail, you can usually pick it up again by heading toward the ridge. About 150 feet after leaving the Crest Trail you enter an aspen grove (wp NPKWP2), which will confirm that you've taken the correct path. The hike to North Peak is 0.4 mile from this spot.

The trail swings to the west and climbs toward the peak. About 0.1 mile from your destination, the trail cuts through a rocky clearing. If you lose the trail, head to the mountain's bare rim on your left and continue uphill. You will see stunning views to the south of Sandia Crest from here.

North Sandia Peak is reached a short distance later (wp NRTHPK). It is marked by a couple of old cement foundation blocks. These pads formed the foundation of a signaling beacon to warn airplanes away during World War II. A similar structure was in place on South Sandia Peak through the early 1960s, and the concrete base pads are still present today.

Extending your hike: Most people will want to end their hike at North Peak. However, a very rough path leads down to the Knife Edge of the Shield. The trail drops about four hundred feet in elevation through tree cover and rock ledges. The path is faint to nonexistent and involves many rock scrambles requiring both hands to proceed. Near the end of this route, the tree cover disappears, and the path levels out over soft ground. It then turns to sheer rock farther to the west when you've reached the Knife Edge of the Shield (wp SHLDKE). There are spectacular views all around. Enjoy the scenery, but go no farther. Only experienced rock climbers should go out onto the Knife Edge because of eleven-hundred-foot sheer dropoffs on either side. Make your way back up to North Sandia Peak by retracing your route to the east.

Capulin Peak Trail

Length: 0.5 mile (one way)
Elevation: 8,740–8,929 feet
Rating: Easy
See Map: 3 (page 40)
Driving Instructions: To reach the trailhead for this hike, head east from Albuquerque on I-40, north on NM 14 for six miles and up the Crest Highway (NM 536) eight miles to Capulin Spring Snow Play Area, which is marked by signs, and take the turnoff. When you pull off the Crest Highway, take the first right onto a narrow, curving road. Follow this road as it becomes one lane, until it dead ends in a small circular turnaround (wp CAPSTH).

Description

This is a short hike to Capulin Peak that follows a popular cross-country ski trail. It is a cool, quick hike that you can enjoy during the summer months; it will be snow packed and icy during the winter, due to its elevation. You will be rewarded with beautiful views of the mountain's eastern slopes from atop Capulin Peak. *Capulin* is Spanish for "chokecherry," a shrub found in damp thickets that bears bitter, astringent fruit; hence the name of the plant.

Capulin Spring (wp CAPSPR) is just to the west (uphill) from the parking area. The spring flows out of a PVC pipe into a 25'-long hollowed-out log spillway, then down to a streambed. An underground holding tank surrounded by a chain-link fence is above the spring.

Capulin Peak Trail runs north from the parking area, and it follows a worn path across a small meadow. A hundred yards north of the parking lot is a set of about a dozen two-foot-tall posts, resembling traffic barriers (wp CAPSW1). The trail goes uphill through this series of barriers, and it crosses some flat, wide rocks. Hike uphill for about a tenth of a mile, then, shortly after crossing under the power lines, the trail dead ends into a "T" with another trail going east-west (wp CAPSW2). There should be a blue diamond sign (cross-country ski marker) with a yellow arrow pointing left and right. Take the right (east) branch and continue on the trail marked by blue diamonds. After a hundred yards or so, the trail splits into a "Y" (wp CAPSW3) Go to the **left** branch; the right (southeast) branch heads back under the power lines and doesn't lead to Capulin Peak.

Follow this left branch for a few hundred yards until the trail appears to dead end on a rise (wp CAPSW4). The trail continues from here, but heads ninety degrees to the right (going southeast). It passes prospecting holes from past mining activity. Purple crystals of fluorite (also called fluorspar, CaF_2) can be found in some of these prospect holes.

You can follow the rocky path to Capulin Peak itself (wp CAPSW5). It is well worth going all of the way to the peak. The peak is so flat that it is hard to discern, and it is only 0.1 mile from the ninety-degree turn. Capulin Peak was the site of an early Forest Service tower used as a fire-warning lookout. The tower burned down in 1948, and a few signs of the base structure remain.

There are beautiful views of the eastern slopes of the Sandias, as well as the ski area to the south. It makes a great spot for lunch. Enjoy the scenery and return to your car by the route you walked up. Many worn paths crisscross the area, so be careful to return in the right direction.

Survey Trail

Length: 2.8 miles (one way)
Elevation: 9,820–10,400 feet
Rating: Moderate
See Map: 5 (page 46)
Driving Instructions: To find the trailhead, go east on I-40 from Albuquerque, north on NM 14 for six miles. Take the Crest Highway (NM 536) 12.1 miles and park at the Ellis Trail parking lot on the south side of the road, marked by a sign (wp ELISPK).

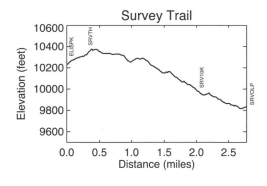

Description

Survey Trail, a cross-country ski trail marked with blue diamond signs, is easy to follow. During the summer months it is a cool and lush hike. The elevation change is modest, and almost anyone can hike it. It receives a "Moderate" rating only because of its length if you chose to hike its entire span. This trail will be inaccessible during winter months because of snow pack.

It is a bit hard to find Survey Trail itself, so here's what I do. From the Ellis Trail parking area, walk north on the Crest Highway for 0.4 miles (wp SRVTH). On the right (east) side of the road, there should be a tree with a number of different four-inch metal signs (for example, a blue diamond, a white square with a symbol of a skier, a yellow square, and a black diamond with a white curvy line) marking the entrance into the woods. Enter the tree-covered area, and begin following the trail north.

Survey Trail is flat, wide, and shaded. It is similar to the more heavily traveled 10K Trail, which is to the east about a half mile. Survey Trail is one of the most pleasant hikes in the Sandias. The first part of the trail heading north parallels the Crest Highway, which is less than one hundred yards above you. Your path crosses under the power lines after a third of a mile on the trail (wp SRVPWR). The trail continues with a slight downhill grade going north, and eventually crosses 10K Trail, marked by a gray sign pole (wp SRV10K). Continuing north, you will reach the junction with Osha Loop Trail about 0.75 mile later (wp SRVOLP). This intersection marks the northern end of Survey Trail.

To finish the hike, retrace your steps south to the Crest Highway. Survey Trail continues for a short distance on the opposite side of the road. If you would rather walk back to your car through the woods, cross the road and look for a continuation of the trail, which is marked by a blue diamond sign. Beware that this area is crisscrossed with many other marked and unmarked cross-country ski trails. Follow trails that roughly parallel the highway for about a half mile, and you should come out on the dirt service road just south of the Ellis parking lot.

Extending your hike: From the northern end of Survey Trail, one option is the three-mile circuit around Osha Loop Trail (with a final half mile on 10K Trail to take you back to Survey Trail).

Boundary Loop Route

Length: 2.5 miles (round trip)
Elevation: 6,100–6,620 feet
Rating: Moderate
See Map: 21 (page 135)
Driving Instructions: Take Tramway Blvd. one mile north of the Tram and turn east onto FR 333. Park at small lot past the second cattle guard 0.3 mile east of the turnoff from Tramway. The trail begins on the north side of FR 333 (wp BNDTH).

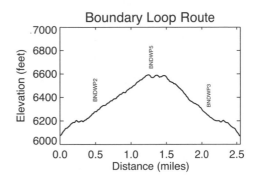

Description

This hike takes you through Jaral Canyon, a little-traveled area in the western foothills. Although I refer to this hike as Boundary Loop Route, the two branches forming the loop are alternately known as East Jaral Canyon Trail (No. 204) and West Jaral Canyon Trail (No. 3A). The area is outside the Sandia Mountain Wilderness, so mountain biking is allowed. It is a good, short hike when you want to get out for a bit of exercise. However, because of the lack of shade it can also be quite hot.

Boundary Loop Route starts up a rocky slope north of FR 333, which leads to the ridge. Just over the ridgeline, the trail takes a turn to the right and then follows a contour eastward. After about a half mile, the trail makes a sharp dip (wp BNDWP1). From here, Boundary Loop Route goes north; another trail (No, 3A) leads south over the ridge.

Go north for about two hundred yards, up the broad arroyo along a fairly well-worn trail. A trail then veers to the east (wp BNDWP3). Follow this path to a blind opening into a rugged arroyo (wp BNDWP2) with large rocks at the mouth of the entrance. A few yards later, you will have to scramble up a five-foot-high rock bed that blocks the way. If you find these landmarks, you are in the proper entrance to the eastern portion of the Boundary Loop Route (Trail 204). From here, continue to hike up the streambed for about a mile until you reach the northern end of the trail. At the northern end of Jaral Canyon, hike up a slope to reach an overlook (wp BNDWP4) above the deep Juan Tabo Canyon to the north. (That area contains several trails that are described in the hike titled "Juan Tabo Canyon.")

From this point, Boundary Loop Route continues up the ridge to the west. After a few minutes, you will reach the top of the ridge (wp BNDWP5), and the trail then starts down another ridge toward the south. Going down, you will arrive at a saddle point where three trails branch (wp BNDWP6). One trail travels to your right, heading north and a little downhill. This trail wraps around the hillside toward the east, and then it makes a steep trip down the hillside all the way into Juan Tabo Canyon and the streambed below (wp BNDTR4). From the three-way junction looking south, the trail before you splits in two. The left branch heads south and up to the ridge that separates the two branches of Jaral Canyon. The right fork continues south, but it drops to the arroyo bottom. This right branch is West Jaral Canyon Trail (Trail No. 3A). Follow that trail as it travels south and generally stays above and to the west of the streambed. Eventually, the trail takes you down into the arroyo bottom (wp BNDWP3). Continuing south for 0.1 mile, you are back at the point where the first part of the Boundary Loop Trail makes the sharp dip downward, as mentioned in the second paragraph of the "Description" (wp BNDWP1).

Extending your hike: From this spot, you can either retrace your path along the beginning of the hike, or you can continue south over the ridge, following the trail down to Forest Road 333. If you choose the latter route, you will find yourself a quarter of a mile from the ruins of Juan Tabo Cabin (wp JTBCAB). See the description of Juan Tabo Cabin Trail for more information about the area. I recommend the short walk to see the cabin and then hiking west along the arroyo to return to your car.

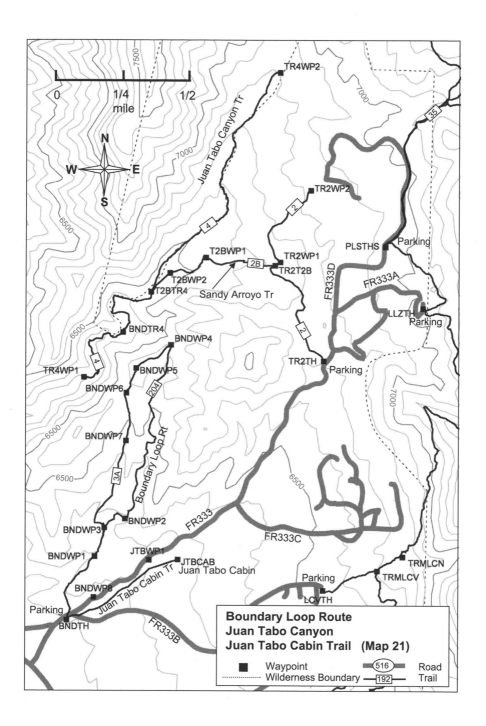

Boundary Loop Route
Juan Tabo Canyon
Juan Tabo Cabin Trail (Map 21)

■ Waypoint ◦◦◦516◦◦◦ Road
⋯⋯ Wilderness Boundary —192— Trail

Juan Tabo Canyon

Length: 6.5 miles (total distance of hike described below)
Elevation: 6,240–6,830 feet
Rating: Moderate
See Map: 21 (page 135)
Driving Instructions: Take Tramway Blvd. one mile north of the turnoff to the Tram, and turn east onto FR 333. After 1.6 miles there is a small dirt parking area on the north side of the road (wp TR2TH). There are also a couple of small parking spaces just past this area on the south side of the road.

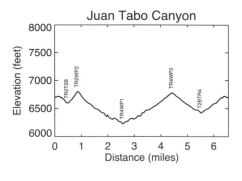

Description

This is a seldom hiked area of the mountain in Juan Tabo Canyon. The trails covered in this hike are Trail No. 2 (Old CCC Loop Trail), No. 2B (Sandy Arroyo Trail), and No. 4 (Juan Tabo Canyon Trail). This is a great fall or winter outing; it is a very hot hike in the summer months.

From the parking area, begin the hike on Trail 2, which is well worn and broad. The trail travels uphill from the parking area for a short way and then down into Juan Tabo Canyon. As the trail turns to the west, it begins to parallel a streambed. About a third of a mile from the trailhead, the trail drops into a sandy arroyo. This is the intersection with Trail No. 2B, the Sandy Arroyo Trail (wp TR2T2B). However, before hiking Trail 2B, I suggest staying on Trail 2 and hiking to its end.

To continue on Trail 2, which goes north from this spot, take a right turn into the arroyo and walk north for about fifty yards (wp TR2WP1). Look for a distinct, well-worn trail going off to the west and uphill, which is the continuation of Trail 2. This stretch of trail makes a steady climb. There are beautiful views of the western, rocky face of the Sandias looming high above to the east, and the green Rincon area to the north. You can follow Trail 2 about a quarter of a mile to its end (wp TR2WP2), which is barricaded. The path actually continues uphill, but it leads to private property in a residential area, so go no farther. Hiking back down the trail, you will see a huge hole in the wall forming the southwest rim of Juan

Tabo Canyon. That landmark is your next destination. First, retrace your steps to the sandy arroyo (wp TR2T2B).

Walk down Sandy Arroyo Trail (marked No. 2B on the map) and head southwest by following the arroyo. There will be lots of footprints from previous hikers, but this is not a maintained trail. After about a quarter of a mile (wp T2BWP1), the arroyo makes a forty-five degree turn south, and the path becomes indistinct. A short distance later (wp T2BWP2), it makes another turn to the left, and you begin hiking south. After a few more minutes, the trail merges into an arroyo coming down from the north. This spot is the junction (wp T2BTR4) with the Juan Tabo Canyon Trail (No. 4 on the map), running north-south. (You will be returning to this spot twice on later legs of this hike, so take a good look and memorize the landmarks here.)

Follow the arroyo and Juan Tabo Canyon Trail (No. 4) to the south, in a streambed through a number of twists into the canyon. There is usually flowing water for the second half of this short distance. In this scenic canyon, you may feel a bit isolated and penned-in. I don't recommend going back into the area alone.

The stream and canyon eventually run into a fence, which marks the boundary with the Sandia Pueblo grounds (wp TR4WP1). No trespassing is allowed onto the tribal land. At the southern end of Trail No. 4, retrace your steps 0.8 miles back up the trail to the intersection with Trail No. 2B.

It can be difficult to find the turnoff going up the northern half of Juan Tabo Canyon Trail No. 4 unless you are using a GPS. From the south end of Trail 4, as you walk out of the last tight canyon into the broader and open area of Juan Tabo Canyon, look for two landmarks. The first, which is quite obvious, is the steep canyon wall looming hundreds of feet overhead in front of you and to your left (the western rim of this large canyon). Juan Tabo Canyon Trail continues up the arroyo just to the east of this steep slope. The second landmark that you see when heading up from the southern end of the trail is a much smaller mound (maybe forty feet high) in front of you and a little to the east of the arroyo. Juan Tabo Canyon Trail (No. 4) heads to the west of the small mound; Sandy Arroyo Trail (No. 2B) heads east, just south of the mound. With these landmarks in mind, keep a sharp eye out for a "Y" in the trail heading north (wp T2BTR4), and you should be able to find the northern branch of Juan Tabo Canyon Trail by taking the left branch at this

"Y." (This is your second of three passes through this junction, wp T2BTR4.)

You can hike the north portion of Trail 4 for about a mile to reach its northern terminus. This section of the trail is also quite sandy, but you should be able to follow foot tracks the entire way. At the northern end, the trail passes the backyard of a private residence just before the arroyo curves to the right (east). The trail ends at a fence marking the boundary of private property (wp TR4WP2).

To return to your car, hike back south on Juan Tabo Canyon Trail and pick up Sandy Arroyo Trail No. 2B heading back east at the now familiar trail junction (wp T2BTR4). Follow the arroyo east to the intersection with Trail No. 2 (wp TR2T2B), and walk south out of the arroyo to the parking area (wp TR2TH).

Juan Tabo Cabin Trail

Length: 0.5 mile (one way)
Elevation: 6,120–6,380 feet
Rating: Easy
See Map: 21 (page 135)
Driving Instructions: Take Tramway Blvd. (NM 556) one mile north of the turnoff to the Sandia Peak Aerial Tramway and then turn east onto FR 333. Park on the right side of the road (wp BNDTH) immediately after crossing the second cattle guard (0.3 mile from Tramway Blvd.). Alternate parking is 0.3 miles farther up FR 333 on the right side (wp JTBWP1), which is only 200 yards or so from the cabin.

Description
Juan Tabo Cabin is an historic landmark at the western foot of the Sandias. It was headquarters for a Civilian Conservation Corps camp that included a number of buildings back in the 1930s. Workers lived in the camp while constructing projects in the area, including the La Cueva and Juan Tabo picnic grounds. The ruins of the cabin are visible from FR 333.

From the parking area, walk a short distance east to FR 333B, which branches to your right. The rough trail heads northeast along the sandy arroyo (that FR 333B crosses after fifty yards). This route is popular with horseback riders as well as hikers. The trail snakes its way up the arroyo through chamisa and junipers toward Juan Tabo Cabin. Here are great views of the brown rolling hills that form the southern rim of Jaral Canyon to the north, and the sheer granite western face of the Sandias before you. After 0.4 mile a worn path on firmer ground veers off to your right and leads to the cabin. A rugged old stone staircase goes up to the ruins of Juan Tabo Cabin.

The cabin, surrounded by a low perimeter wall, consisted of three rooms. The roof was destroyed in a fire long ago. Two stone benches are built into the outside wall on either side of the entry doorway and face west. This makes a pleasant place to sit and enjoy the sunset year round.

Fig. 20. Juan Tabo Cabin.

Rincon Spur Trail

Length: 0.8 mile (one way)
Elevation: 8,200–8,500 feet
Rating: Moderate
See Map: 11 (page 86)
Driving Instructions: You access Rincon Spur Trail from the south Piedra Lisa Trail trailhead. Take Tramway Boulevard one mile north of the turnoff to the Tram and then turn east onto FR 333. After about two miles, where FR 333 takes a right turn through a stone gate, go straight ahead on FR 333D, which becomes a dirt road. Continue a short distance along the dirt road to the Piedra Lisa Trail parking lot (wp PLSTHS).

Description

The Rincon forms a prominent ridge extending west from the base of the Shield and then turning south. The *Rincon* is aptly named—Spanish for "corner." Looking east from the intersection of I-25 and Tramway Blvd., you will see a huge hole notched into the southwest section of the Rincon ridge by Juan Tabo Canyon.

Rincon Spur Trail is a short, unmaintained hiking route that runs east and west along the Rincon. It is most easily accessed by hiking about two miles north on Piedra Lisa Trail from its south trailhead; see the discussion of Piedra Lisa Trail for more information about trail access. Signs mark the Piedra Lisa Trail at the top of the ridge (wp PLSWP1), which is the beginning point for the hike along the Rincon Spur Trail.

As noted elsewhere, the region east of Piedra Lisa Trail and south of the Rincon officially closes to the public between March 1 and August 15 every year. However, the eastern portion of the Rincon Spur Trail remains open. This branch of the trail travels to the base of the Shield rock formation. It is often used by rock climbers for access to the Knife Edge of the Shield and to the Shield's north face or the west end of the south face. Most of this route is well worn and easy to follow, but it is steep in some places.

Hike east along the ridge from Piedra Lisa Trail (wp PLSWP1). The trickiest part comes about two hundred yards into this route. The trail is blocked by some large rocks, perhaps forty feet high (wp RSPWP1). To continue east you must scramble up the smooth rock about ten feet. Once atop these rocks, you will see the trail continuing in front of you and a little to the left (to the northeast). Scramble ten or fifteen feet down to the other side of the rocks and pick up the trail again. Once past this obstacle, the Rincon Spur is again easy to follow. About 250 yards later, you cross a nice saddle point along the ridge, which is quite narrow at this point (wp RSPWP2). The trail continues on a bit more, and then drops down thirty or forty feet at the base of the Shield's Knife Edge (wp RSPWP3). Rock climbers begin the ascent of the Knife Edge from here; crude paths to the right give access to the southwest face of the Shield.

Another path continues to the left from here, around the corner and back above the south fork of Del Agua Canyon (to the north). You can follow the trail into this canyon for a while longer and will be rewarded with beautiful views to the northwest. However, the trail soon narrows and starts appearing hazardous (wp RSPWP4). I would suggest that only the most adventurous hikers go farther. I usually turn around here and retrace my steps to Piedra Lisa Trail.

From Piedra Lisa Trail at the ridgeline (wp PLSWP1) another branch of the Rincon Spur Trail goes west. The trail to the west, along level ground, is quite well worn and pleasant. You can follow the trail for about a quarter of a mile until it makes a steep dropoff (wp RSPWP5). Notice the beautiful views to the south, across Juan Tabo Canyon. Farther progress west along the Rincon Spur Trail is possible, but difficult, and I usually turn around here.

Fletcher Trail

Length: 2 miles (one way)
Elevation: 6,930–8,220 feet
Rating: Moderate
See Map: 11 (page 86)
Driving Instructions: Take Tramway Boulevard one mile north of the turnoff to the Tram, and then turn east onto FR 333. After two miles, pass the turnoff to La Luz Trail (that way is marked as FR 333), and continue straight ahead, on the dirt road marked as FR 333D. The dirt road turns right around a corner and leads back to the Piedra Lisa Trail parking lot (wp PLSTHS).

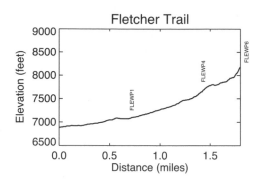

Note: Fletcher Trail and the surrounding area are closed to protect sensitive wildlife areas between March 1 and August 15 every year. Please visit the trail accordingly.

Description

Fletcher Trail is accessed from Piedra Lisa Trail. Fletcher Trail is not part of the maintained trail system in the Sandia Mountains. However, it is well traveled and not hard to follow. The trail is named for Royce Fletcher, who created the trail in 1980.

Hike north from the Piedra Lisa parking lot on the dirt road for about a quarter of a mile until you reach Piedra Lisa Trail, marked by a sign (wp PLSWP4). Piedra Lisa Trail climbs a low ridge and then drops into the streambed of Juan Tabo Canyon, which contains Fletcher Trail, Movie Trail, and Waterfall Canyon—all coming down from the east and intersecting at the bottom of this dip (wp FLETH). Two arroyos run down the mountain from the east, join at this point, and cross Piedra Lisa Trail. The northern arroyo leads to Upper Juan Tabo Canyon via Fletcher Trail. The southern streambed leads up Waterfall Canyon. The trail on the ridge between these two canyons is described in the hike titled "Movie Trail."

Begin Fletcher Trail by hiking up the north arroyo. You should see a wooden sign a short distance up the trail that contains the seasonal closure warning, mentioned above (wp FLEWP1). About a half mile up Fletcher Trail, the trail lifts out of the sandy arroyo, onto the east bank (wp FLEWP3). This turnoff is easy to miss, so keep a close eye for it (or use the GPS waypoint). From this spot, Fletcher Trail heads into the woods, and it becomes a pleasant walk. The trail parallels the arroyo for about a third of a mile, swings north and crosses the arroyo (wp FLEWP2), and then heads east up to a ridge.

The steep hike up the ridge has poor footing because of the loose dirt. After topping this ridge, the trail turns south (wp FLEWP4) and then swings east, going back into a canyon. There are beautiful views of the Prow (rock formation) to the south across this canyon. Eventually, you will come to the base of an obvious large rock formation, which is UNM Spire (wp FLEWP5). This is a fine spot to end your hike for the day. Going farther will involve scrambling up some loose rocks.

If you decide to go a little farther, the trail continues south around the corner of the slope, below large rock formations and toward some dripping springs. The scrambling on the trail becomes difficult, and the trail becomes fainter. Eventually, you will reach a slope of loose rocks and you must scramble ten or fifteen feet up the base of another large rock formation with a dripping spring overhead. (wp FLEWP6). The rock face above has mottled black stains from lichen. This quiet, isolated spot creates a sublime ending to Fletcher Trail. (Experienced rock climbers often go on from here, dropping down twenty or thirty feet and bushwhacking to the base of a rock formation called the Ramp.) From the dripping spring, retrace your steps along Fletcher Trail to your car.

Movie Trail

Length: 1.7 miles (one way)
Elevation: 6,930–8,370 feet
Rating: Moderate
See Map: 11 (page 86)
Driving Instructions: Take Tramway Boulevard one mile north of the turnoff to the Tram and then turn east onto FR 333. After two miles, pass the turnoff to La Luz Trail (that way is marked as FR 333), and continue straight ahead, on the dirt road marked as FR 333D. The dirt road turns right around a corner and leads to the Piedra Lisa Trail parking lot (wp PLSTHS).

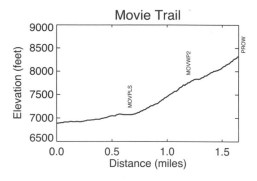

Note: Movie Trail and the surrounding area are closed to protect sensitive wildlife areas from March 1 to August 15 every year.

Description

Movie Trail is not an official part of the trail system maintained by the Forest Service. As such, it is indistinct to nonexistent in many places. Navigation of the route with a GPS may be helpful. The trail was built in the early 1960s for filming of the movie *Lonely are the Brave*, starring Kirk Douglas.

Hike north from the Piedra Lisa parking lot along the dirt road for about a quarter of a mile until you reach Piedra Lisa Trail, marked by a sign (wp PLSWP4). Piedra Lisa Trail passes over a rise, then drops into a small canyon that contains Fletcher Trail, Movie Trail, and Waterfall Canyon, all coming down from the east and intersecting at the bottom of this dip (wp FLETH). Two arroyos dropping down the mountain from the east cross Piedra Lisa Trail. The northern arroyo leads to Upper Juan Tabo Canyon via Fletcher Trail. The southern streambed leads up Waterfall Canyon. Movie Trail runs along the ridge between these two canyons.

To find the start of Movie Trail, walk up the south streambed for about twenty yards, then veer off to the left at about a forty-five-degree angle. Follow a small dry gully up and to the left. Movie Trail goes up the ridgeline from here on a loose dirt path. The footing is not good, so please be careful. The steep portion of the trail is only about a quarter mile long, so take heart. From the top of the ridge (wp MOVWP1), the trail heads southward, but generally it becomes hard to discern.

With or without a trail, you must make your way up the hill and to the north, toward the ridgeline and a small plateau (wp MOVWP2); this is one place were the GPS waypoint may prove quite helpful in navigating the route. From here, make your way north and slightly east to a ridgeline, which will continue all the way to the Prow. Along the way, you should cross a saddle point (wp MOVWP3). It is steep scrambling up rocks for the last few minutes to make your way to the base of the Prow. Enjoy a breathtaking view from the Prow before retracing your steps to the parking area.

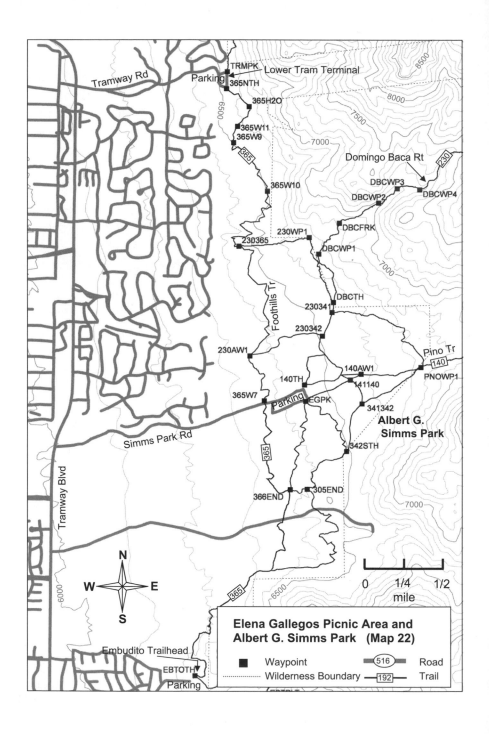

Elena Gallegos Picnic Area and
Albert G. Simms Park (Map 22)

■ Waypoint ▭516▭ Road
········· Wilderness Boundary ▭192▭ Trail

Elena Gallegos Picnic Area and Albert G. Simms Park

Length: Varies with route
Elevation: 6,200–6,700 feet
Rating: Easy
See Map: 22 (page 146)
Driving Instructions: Go north on Tramway Blvd. from Academy, and turn east to the Elena Gallegos Picnic Area on Simms Park Road, marked by signs. You have to pay for parking at the guard station, one dollar on weekdays, and two dollars on weekends. The area is open from 7 A.M. to 7 P.M. in the winter and 7 A.M. to 9 P.M. in the summer, seven days a week. Trail maps of the park are available from the attendant.

Description

The Elena Gallegos Picnic Area, Albert G. Simms Park offers a wonderful outdoor-recreation space at the foot of Pino Canyon in the eastern Sandia Mountain foothills. The area is available to hikers, joggers, mountain bike riders, bird watchers, and artists. Picnic tables, group reservation areas, and restroom facilities are available.

The original Spanish land grant for this area was awarded to Captain Diego Montoya in 1694. Elena Gallegos, his niece, inherited the 35,084-acre parcel of land stretching from the Rio Grande to Sandia Crest around 1716. The land passed down through her descendants for over two centuries. The State of New Mexico claimed eighteen thousand acres for unpaid taxes in the 1920s. Albert G. Simms purchased this land in 1934 for one dollar an acre. When Mr. Simms died in 1964, he left thirteen thousand acres of the land to the Albuquerque Academy. The Academy subsequently sold 7,700 acres to the City of Albuquerque in 1980. Most of this land was traded to the federal government, but 640 acres were set aside to form the Elena Gallegos Picnic Area and Albert G. Simms Park in 1984.

There are a dozen or more multiple-use trails designed for foot, bike, and horse travel in the area. It can be hiked year round. It is an especially great place to exercise during the winter months, when the upper mountain is snow covered. It is busy with mountain bike traffic year round, so be alert and yield the right-of-way to riders. By combining the trails, you can form any number of easy loop hikes.

Piedra Lisa Canyon

Length: 2.5 miles (total distance for hike described below)
Elevation: 6,000–7,200 feet
Rating: Moderate
See Map: 15 (page 106)
Driving Instructions: To find the trailhead, take Candelaria Blvd. east from Tramway Blvd. until it terminates at Camino de la Sierra. Turn south on Camino de la Sierra, and park in the Open Space lot (wp PLCYPK).

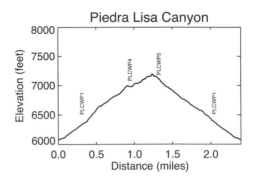

Description

Piedra Lisa Canyon creates a distinctive landmark on the west side of the Sandia Mountains. A large, gray rock formation a couple of hundred feet above the canyon entrance is very noticeable as you drive east on Menaul or Candelaria Blvds. *Piedra lisa* is Spanish for "smooth" or "slick rock," and the canyon is named for this large rock formation. Note that Piedra Lisa Canyon is many miles south of the Piedra Lisa Trail (which is north of La Luz Trail).

Apart from the lower portion of this hike, there are not any well-defined trails in the upper part of Piedra Lisa Canyon. It is relatively easy to find volunteer trails and to make your way through the area. However, because these trails are not developed or maintained, be aware of safety and take precautions. I suggest this hike as a convenient one for getting some exercise during the cold months. Because of its lack of shade, a hike up the western foothills can be quite hot much of the rest of the year.

From the parking lot (wp PLCYPK), hike east toward the large gray rock formation in the canyon straight ahead. There is a trail of sorts along the south side of the canyon to scramble up. Make your way to the gray rock at the top; this rock forms a natural dam near the top the canyon (wp PLCWP1).

From here, there are indistinct trails leading up the north side of the canyon. You can climb up several ridges in that direction to get a good

Fig. 21. Large natural dam in Piedra Lisa Canyon.

workout, and you will be rewarded with beautiful views of the city to the west. The edge of the Sandia Mountain Wilderness lies just to the east, and you may see a downed fence marking the boundary (wp PLCWP3). From these upper ridges (wp PLCWP4) you can make your way south or east.

I often hike the route south to the eastern end of Piedra Lisa Canyon. I then drop down to the streambed (wp PLCWP5), and follow it west to the mouth of the canyon, at the large gray rock (wp PLCWP1). There is some scrambling to do along the way, but it is not too hard. In the winter, there may be ice in parts of the streambed, which can make the footing treacherous. From the top of the natural dam, take the rough path down the south side of the streambed, and make your way back to the parking lot (wp PLCYPK).

Another alternative is to continue east up the main ridge (from wp PLCWP4) about eleven hundred feet in elevation to join Whitewash Trail (at wp WHWWP2). From there, you can take Whitewash Trail down the mountain to form a nice loop. This route will take you to the Menaul parking area, or you can work your way north toward the Open Space parking lot (wp PLCYPK) by cutting cross country near the bottom.

Whitewash Trail

Length: 4 miles (one way)
Elevation: 5,900–8,520 feet
Rating: Difficult
See Map: 15 (page 106)
Driving Instructions: Drive east from Tramway Blvd. on Menaul until it ends at a paved parking area (wp MENLPK).

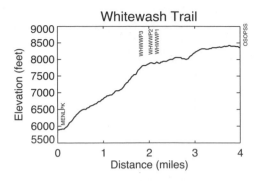

Description

The large gray rock formation at the lower portion of Piedra Lisa Canyon, on a line east from Candelaria Blvd., is known by many locals as "the Whitewash." (The canyon itself is also referred to by some as Whitewash Canyon.) Whitewash Trail travels up the steep mountainside, passing above the canyon and then east to Oso Pass. Although not part of the officially recognized system of trails, Whitewash Trail gets quite a bit of travel.

The lowest portion of Whitewash Trail is a little hard to find. If you look toward the southeast from the Menaul parking area, you will see a long ridgeline rising in silhouette about two hundred yards away. Whitewash Trail generally follows that ridge. Hike to the base of the ridge and look for a rough path ascending the slope. Be careful on the hike up Whitewash Trail. In many places the path consists of fine, loose pebbles as it goes up. The trail gains five hundred feet elevation in the first half mile. At the top of this first stretch, the trail swings north and then begins another steep ascent up the slope. The area is crisscrossed with game trails and other hiking routes. If you seem to lose sight of the trail, keep heading up and to the northeast, and the competing routes eventually consolidate into one.

The trail continues its steep route up the ridge and finally into the tree line. By two miles into the hike, the trail has gained two thousand feet in elevation. After one steep, slick stretch, the trail takes a sharp turn to the north and goes over a forty-foot-high lookout mound (wp WHWWP3). The views are spectacular from the top of this local peak. It is also a nice spot for a well-deserved rest and snack after your climb up the steep mountainside. When hiking down Whitewash Trail, it is particularly easy to lose the trail at the southern base of this mound. The trail makes a sharp turn to the west at that point. I'm sure that I've missed this turn a half dozen times over the years.

Whitewash Trail leads north for about 0.2 mile, and then makes an abrupt bend to the east (wp WHWWP2). On a hike down Whitewash Trail, this sharp turn in the trail can also cause trouble. It is easy to miss the turn and continue straight ahead, following an alternate path down the ridge toward the northwest. If you mistakenly follow the ridge down the mountain, you will exit the mountain near Montgomery Blvd., about two miles north of your car. (Let's just say that I know firsthand how frustrating this can be, and leave it at that.)

The remainder of the route continues eastward to Oso Pass, about two miles away. It is a beautiful hike through the ponderosa pines of the Transition life zone. The route is relatively easy to follow all of the way to Oso Pass (wp OSOPSS).

Extending your hike: From Oso Pass you have many hiking options. Embudito Trail leads north, down the mountain; it also heads east to the South Sandia Peak area. Three Gun Spring Trail travels south from Oso Pass, meeting Embudo Trail after about 1.5 miles. In fact, my favorite loop hike in the Sandias is to hike up Embudo Trail to Three Gun Spring Trail, then over to Oso Pass, and back down the mountain on Whitewash Trail. The complete circuit is about a ten-mile hike.

South Sandia Peak

Length: 0.5 mile (one way, from Embudito Trail)
Elevation: 9,762 feet
Rating: Moderate
See Map: 23 (page 154)
Driving Instructions: See driving instructions to the lower trailheads for the trails approaching South Peak.

Description

South Sandia Peak is the highest point of the southern half of the Sandia Mountains. A series of long, beautiful meadows line the mountain near South Peak. It is a gorgeous area for a day's outing and picnic.

This area can be reached via many different routes, but all involve at least a four-mile hike. There isn't an officially maintained trail to the peak, but at least two good routes can take you there. Instead of describing the area repeatedly with the discussion of each of the access trails, the South Peak area is described separately here.

One approach to South Peak is from the west. Three Gun Spring Trail, Embudito Trail, and Embudo Trail (combined with a 1.5 mile stretch of Three Gun Spring Trail) all lead to Oso Pass (wp OSOPSS), which is below and to the west of South Peak. No matter which of these approaches is taken, it is a four- to five-mile hike to Oso Pass. Embudito Trail continues on a steep climb to the east from Oso Pass. About one mile from Oso Pass, Embudito Trail makes a sharp turn to the east from its southerly course. About 500 feet (0.1 mile) farther east, a spur trail branches to your left leading to South Peak (wp EBTWP4). The turnoff to this path can be hard to spot because of thick, low brush. It is often marked with a cairn, but don't rely on it. The path heads to the northwest, up the slope toward South Peak. After a short steep section, the trail stays just to the west of the ridgeline and crosses a pleasant meadow. After about one-half mile (wp EBTWP5), the path takes a turn to the east for a final scramble up some rocks to the summit of South Peak (wp STHPK).

South Peak can also be approached from the southeast using the Crest Trail. It is about a six-mile hike from the Canyon Estates trailhead to the junction with Embudito Trail (wp SCREBT). A quicker alternative is to take the CCC Route (from its origin near the junction of Upper Faulty and

Fig. 22. Granite buttresses near South Sandia Peak.

the Crest Trail). This route is steep, but cuts off almost two miles compared to hiking the complete distance along the Crest Trail.

There are a couple of choices for hiking to South Peak from the intersection of Embudito Trail and the Crest Trail. The first is to hike west from this trail junction along Embudito Trail. Within 0.1 mile the trail goes over a ridge and then turns north for a short distance. Embudito Trail then makes a sharp turn to the west (wp EBTWP6). It is easy to miss this turn and to continue north up the slope; indeed a path continues up the slope for a hundred feet or so, I suspect from people who have missed the turn. However, that way is quickly strangled by low brush. Continue west along Embudito Trail for another 250 yards to the side trail turnoff described two paragraphs above (wp EBTWP4). Look for a trail branching to the northwest, and perhaps a rock cairn marking the junction. Follow this trail for half a mile to South Peak, as previously discussed.

A second, and probably better, route from the Embudito–Crest Trail junction (wp SCREBT) is to hike north along the Crest Trail. The Crest Trail runs east of and below the main ridgeline through here. After hiking about

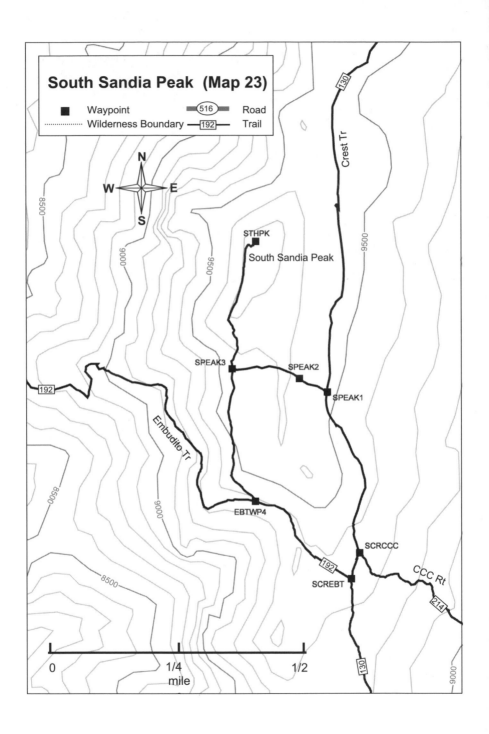

South Sandia Peak (Map 23)

Legend:
- Waypoint
- Wilderness Boundary
- 516 — Road
- 192 — Trail

South Sandia Peak

Crest Tr
Embudito Tr
CCC Rt

STHPK
SPEAK3
SPEAK2
SPEAK1
EBTWP4
SCRCCC
SCREBT

130
192
214

0   1/4   1/2
mile

0.4 mile north from the Embudito Trail junction you will see the ridgeline about 300 yards to the west across a grassy meadow. There is a faint path to the west branching from the Crest Trail, sometimes marked by a cairn (wp SPEAK1). Follow that path or walk cross-country west to the main ridgeline. You should meet a worn path running north-south (wp SPEAK3), which you can follow north to the peak.

Finally, South Peak is often accessed from the north using either Bart's Trail or Cañoncito Trail. From the junction of Bart's Trail and the Crest Trail (wp BRTSCR), South Peak is about 1.5 miles south along the Crest Trail. There is thick tree cover separating the peak from the Crest Trail, so I usually continue south past the peak for another third of a mile (wp SPEAK1), then take a faint path to the west across the open meadow to the ridge-line (wp SPEAK3). From there, follow the worn trail north about three hundred yards to South Peak.

The 360-degree views, remoteness, and hard work required to reach the summit make South Sandia Peak one of the most rewarding destinations in the mountains. I hope that you will enjoy the area as much as I do.

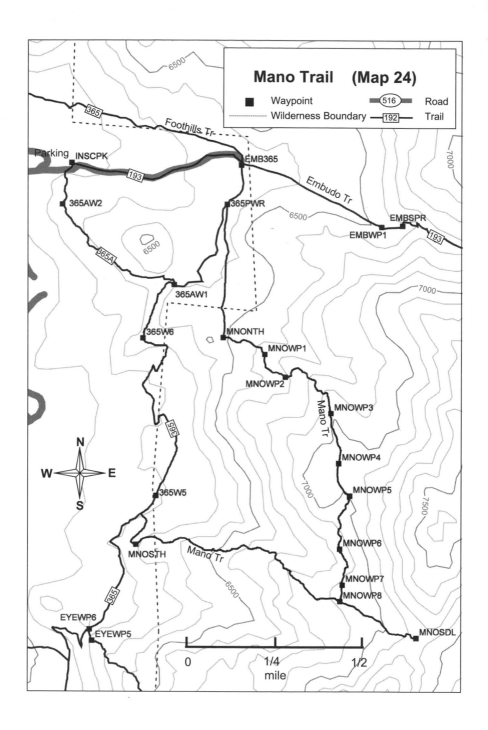

Mano Trail   (Map 24)

■ Waypoint   〈516〉 Road

···· Wilderness Boundary   〔192〕 Trail

6500

365

Foothills Tr

Parking INSCPK

193

EMB365

Embudo Tr

365AW2

365PWR

6500

EMBSPR

EMBWP1

193

7000

365A

6500

365AW1

7000

365W6

MNONTH

MNOWP1

MNOWP2

MNOWP3

Mano Tr

MNOWP4

365

7000

MNOWP5

N

W ⊹ E

S

365W5

7500

MNOWP6

MNOSTH

Mano Tr

MNOWP7

MNOWP8

365

6500

EYEWP6

EYEWP5

MNOSDL

0   1/4   1/2

mile

Mano Trail

Length: 5 miles (total distance for hike described below)
Elevation: 6,180–7,140 feet
Rating: Moderate
See Map: 24 (page 156)
Driving Instructions: From Tramway Blvd., go east on Indian School Road until it ends at a large paved parking area for Embudo Trail (wp INSCPK).

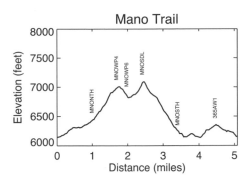

You might consider leaving a second car at the Open Space parking lot at the east end of Copper Blvd. Doing so would shorten the end of this hike by about two miles.

Description

Mano Trail is a lesser-used route in the western foothills at the southern end of the Sandia Mountains. It provides an enjoyable spring, fall, or winter hike, when you want to get outside for a workout. Because of its low elevation and exposure to the sun, Mano Trail can be quite hot in the summer months.

The trail takes its name from a stone artifact that was reportedly found in the area, a "mano." The mano and metate were tools used for grinding corn and other seeds into a powdery meal. *Mano* is the Spanish word for "hand." The hand-held mano was rubbed back and forth across the flat, rough stone metate to grind the material to the desired consistency.

Start this hike by walking east along Embudo Trail, then cut south around the east end of the large flood-control holding pond. It is more efficient to stay on an old rocky path that runs below the power lines (wp 365PWR) than to follow Trail 365 (the Foothills Trail), which veers a little westward. The north trailhead for Mano Trail lies at the base of the third set of power-line poles (three poles side by side), at the top of the second ridge that you will reach (wp MNONTH). From this ridge looking south, you should be able to see the U-Mound a couple of miles to the south. (U-Mound forms a sharply conical hill near the east end of Copper Blvd. The University of New Mexico students used to whitewash a large "U" on the mound, which was visible from most of the city.) There is a wide trail heading east from the power-line poles, which is Mano Trail. There may be a small sign marking the Sandia Mountain Wilderness boundary a few yards up the trail.

The trail is clearly visible and easy to follow up the ridge for a tenth of a mile, or so. Mano Trail then takes a jog south (wp MNOWP1) around the corner of a ridge into a small canyon. Follow the trail back into this canyon (walking east) to the point that the trail starts to swing around in the canyon and turns to the south. Just before the trail swings south, look closely for a branch of the trail going up the hill and to the left (wp MNOWP2). It is easy to miss this turn to the left. Once you've found the correct turnoff, the trail continues northeast up to the top of the ridge-line. At the top of the ridge (wp MNOWP3), the trail is again easy to follow for quite a distance. **Note:** The hardest part of this trail is the turnoff that I just mentioned. If you find yourself in the wrong place, you probably need to go back and navigate that section again.

After a steep climb up the ridge, the trail reaches the top of a wide plateau. There are panoramic views in all directions, including Albuquerque laid out to the west. This flat stretch is quite welcome after the hike up the ridge. The trail continues east, then swings around to the south, going behind a small hill to the west. Behind that hill, piled high with large boulders, is a broad saddle point (wp MNOWP4), after which the trail begins a slight downhill grade.

Continuing to follow the trail, you reach the edge of a canyon to the south (wp MNOWP5). Across this canyon, directly to the south, lies another broad plateau, upon which lies the southern half of Mano Trail. Continue to hike straight south, dropping down about a hundred feet into the canyon (wp MNOWP6), then scramble up the slope on the other side. There is an indistinct trail going straight across this small canyon. Follow it as best you can, coming up on the opposite side (wp MNOWP7). Once on the far side of the canyon, continue walking south on the plateau until you run into a well-worn trail running east-west (wp MNOWP8). This is the southern leg of Mano Trail.

For some distinctive scenery, I recommend following Mano Trail to the east on this plateau, and on to a prominent rise just a quarter of a mile up the hill. There is a single large tree at the top of the saddle point (wp MNOSDL); it is a distinctive landmark that you can see from the streets of Albuquerque, if you know where to look. There are vistas in all directions from this pass, including a view across Echo Canyon to Tijeras

Canyon to the southeast. There are faint volunteer trails heading to the north and to the south from the pass, and going up to the prominent neighboring peaks on either side.

The path west, down the foothills on the southern leg of Mano Trail, is easy to follow. It travels west across the broad plateau below the pass, and generally keeps to the ridgeline as you lose elevation. Mano Trail ends at a set of quadruple power-line poles on top of a ridge (wp MNOSTH). When you reach this spot, you should see U-Mound to the southwest.

If you have left a car at the parking lot off Copper, you can head south from this point on crisscrossing trails that head generally south and east of U-Mound. Once you've passed U-Mound, head around to the west to the Copper parking area.

If your ride is back at the Indian School lot, then head north from Mano Trail, back toward the Embudo trailhead. Traveling north from the ridge, you will pass a large sign (wp 365W5) pointing one direction for the Copper Trailhead and the other direction for Embudo Trailhead. You are now on the Foothills Trail (No. 365). Continue hiking north on this trail. The route generally parallels the power lines that run north-south, but it keeps to the west and a few hundred feet below them most of the way. After about a mile and a half, Trail 365 takes a swing to the east, toward the power lines. This is just north of the set of power-line poles at the northern Mano trailhead (wp MNONTH). Continuing north along Trail 365 would lead you around the east end of the large holding pond that you passed earlier in the hike. However, at this point (wp 365AW1) there is another sign pointing to Trail 365A that continues going north. You can take Trail 365A, which soon wraps around the west side of some hills and drops you down to the Indian School parking area (wp INSCPK). Taking Trail 365A cuts off about half the final distance of the hike.

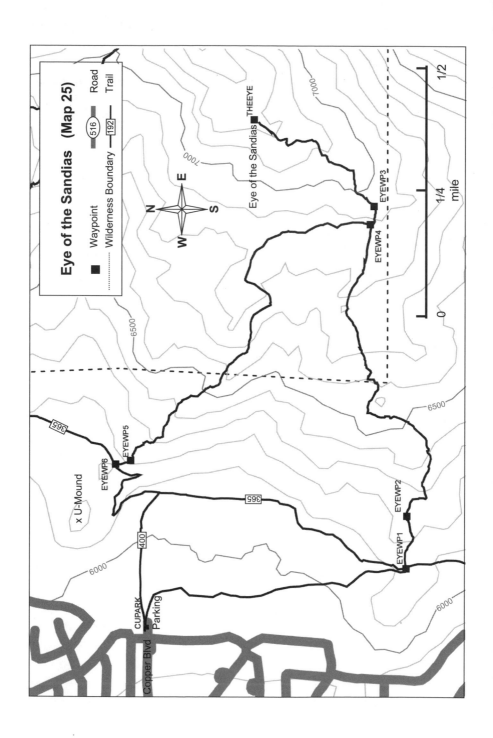

Eye of the Sandias (Map 25)

Road

Trail

Waypoint

Wilderness Boundary

516

192

N

E

S

W

THEEYE

Eye of the Sandias

7000

7000

6500

EYEWP3

EYEWP4

6500

EYEWP5

365

EYEWP6

x U-Mound

EYEWP2

365

EYEWP1

400

6000

6000

CUPARK

Parking

Copper Blvd

0   1/4   1/2

mile

Eye of the Sandias

Length: 4 miles (total distance for hike described below)
Elevation: 5,940–7,200 feet
Rating: Moderate
See Map: 25 (page 160)
Driving Instructions: Drive north from Tramway and Central to Copper, and turn east. Park at the lot at the east end of Copper (wp CUPARK).

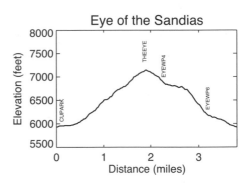

Eye of the Sandias

Description

The Eye of the Sandias is a quirky landmark in the southern foothills of the Sandia Mountains. Painted on a large rock overlooking Tijeras Canyon is a stylized eyeball with two large tears dripping down, and a Zia symbol in the middle of the pupil. The Eye appeared sometime in the 1960s, but the originator is unknown. In the spring of 2002 it was freshly repainted by someone. Urban legend has it that the Eye represents a symbol of sadness and protest at the encroachment of the city on the mountain.

The hike to the Eye makes for a fun outing. This is an ideal hike for the winter months. In summer, the absence of shade may make the route unbearably hot. The distance from the parking lot to The Eye is about two miles, with an elevation gain of around twelve hundred feet. The area is crisscrossed with scores of walking and bicycle paths. If you have a GPS, following the waypoints that are provided below may be the most reliable way to navigate to the Eye.

From the parking area look to the south to find two low distinct hills. Hike to the saddle point between these two hills, about one half mile (wp EYEWP1). At the top of the saddle point, there will be a trail heading east. Follow that trail for most of the rest of the hike. The trail passes underneath a set of power lines shortly east of this saddle point (wp EYEWP2). The trail is more or less distinct in places, but generally it isn't too hard to follow. Eventually it begins to parallel an old barbed-wire fence while keeping to the north side.

Keep following that trail upward, and you should see a turnoff to a ridgeline that runs north-south (wp EYEWP3). From this turnoff, a trail

Fig. 23. The Eye of the Sandias.

heads northeast up the ridgeline toward the Eye. It is a rather steep walk up this final ridge. Just when you are about to get discouraged, you will see the Eye come into view from a hundred yards away. Once you reach the Eye, there are great views of Tijeras Canyon to the south and Albuquerque to the west from this prominent spot (wp THEEYE).

On the way down, I suggest an alternate trail to vary the scenery. Hike back down the final ridge to the turnoff (wp EYEWP3) and begin walking west. About two hundred feet west of that turnoff, look for a trail heading north (wp EYEWP4). This well-worn trail comes out at a set of four power-line poles (wp EYEWP5), just a short distance above the saddle point to the east of U-Mound, and meets the Foothills Trail (No. 365) (wp EYEWP6). Follow Trail 365 south, down the hill through a couple of switchbacks until it meets Trail 400, which goes west to the parking area.

Appendix 1: Summary of Trails

Difficulty	Trail Name	Miles	Elevation Range (feet)	Page
Moderate	Cienega Trail	2.2	7,500–9,220	p. 22
Moderate	Armijo Trail	2.2	7,100–7,230	p. 24
Easy	Sulphur Canyon Trail	0.4	7,420–7,620	p. 27
Easy	Bill Spring Trail	0.7	7,400–7,720	p. 28
Moderate	Faulty Trail	8.7	7,000–7,860	p. 30
Easy	Oso Corredor Trail	2.7	7,810–8,600	p. 33
Moderate	Tree Spring Trail	2.0	8,470–9,440	p. 36
Easy	Tecolote Trail	1.3	8,630–8,810	p. 38
Easy	Balsam Glade Nature Trail	0.3	8,620–8,660	p. 39
Moderate	10K Trail	4.7	9,440–10,040	p. 41
Moderate	Ellis Trail	3.2	9,640–10,270	p. 44
Moderate	Osha Loop Trail	2.4	9,210–9,740	p. 47
Most Difficult	Chimney Canyon Route	1.7	8,150–10,590	p. 49
Easy	Crest Spur Trail	0.6	10,100–10,610	p. 53
Easy	Crest Nature Trail	0.2	10,600	p. 54
Easy	Peak Nature Trail	0.3	10,300	p. 55
Moderate	Peñasco Blanco Trail	1.6	8,450–9,110	p. 57
Easy	Sandia Cave Trail	0.5	7,040–7,180	p. 61
Difficult	Osha Spring Trail	4.3	6,500–9,110	p. 62
Difficult	Crest Trail	26.0	6,240–10,640	p. 64
Difficult	Ojo del Orno Route	0.8	6,400–7,410	p. 72
Difficult	Agua Sarca Route	3.0	6,350–9,040	p. 73
Moderate	Strip Mine Trail	1.8	5,660–6,040	p. 76
Moderate	Del Agua Route	1.8	5,960–7,020	p. 78
Difficult	La Luz Trail	7.5	7,040–10,250	p. 80
Moderate	Piedra Lisa Trail	5.7	6,030–8,150	p. 84
Easy	Piedra Lisa–La Luz Link	0.5	6,960–7,200	p. 88
Easy	La Cueva Trail	0.3	6,500–6,700	p. 89

Difficulty	Trail Name	Miles	Elevation Range (feet)	Page
Easy	Rozamiento Trail	0.6	6,250–6,500	p. 90
Moderate	Tramway Trail	2.5	6,460–7,400	p. 93
Easy	Foothills Trail	13	5,860–6,660	p. 94
Difficult	Domingo Baca Route	3.5	6,450–8,810	p. 97
Moderate	Pino Trail	4.5	6,460–9,230	p. 101
Difficult	Embudito Trail	6.0	6,240–9,400	p. 102
Moderate	Embudo Trail	3.2	6,180–7,860	p. 105
Moderate	Three Gun Spring Trail	4.0	6,320–8,460	p. 108
Moderate	Hawk Watch Trail	2.0	6,300–7,900	p. 111
Difficult	CCC Route	1.8	7,580–9,345	p. 113
Moderate	Cañoncito Trail	3.0	7,310–9,210	p. 116
Moderate	Bart's Trail	2.0	7,300–9,140	p. 119
Moderate	North Mystery Trail	5.2	7,360–8,110	p. 121
Moderate	Palomas Cliffs Trail	1.5	8,010–8,560	p. 125
Moderate	North Sandia Peak	1.8	10,200–10,600	p. 126
Easy	Capulin Peak Trail	0.5	8,740–8,929	p. 130
Moderate	Survey Trail	2.8	9,820–10,400	p. 131
Moderate	Boundary Loop Route	2.5	6,100–6,620	p. 133
Moderate	Juan Tabo Canyon	6.5	6,240–6,830	p. 136
Easy	Juan Tabo Cabin Trail	0.5	6,120–6,380	p. 138
Moderate	Rincon Spur Trail	0.8	8,200–8,500	p. 140
Moderate	Fletcher Trail	2.0	6,930–8,220	p. 142
Moderate	Movie Trail	1.7	6,930–8,370	p. 144
Easy	Elena Gallegos Picnic Area	Varies	6,200–6,700	p. 147
Moderate	Piedra Lisa Canyon	2.5	6,000–7,200	p. 148
Difficult	Whitewash Trail	4.0	5,900–8,520	p. 150
Moderate	South Sandia Peak	0.5	9,762	p. 152
Moderate	Mano Trail	5.0	6,180–7,140	p. 157
Moderate	Eye of the Sandias	4.0	5,940–7,200	p. 161

Appendix 2: Trails Listed by Difficulty

Easy Trails:
Balsam Glade Nature Trail, p. 39
Bill Spring Trail, p. 28
Capulin Peak Trail, p. 130
Crest Nature Trail, p.54
Crest Spur Trail, p. 53
Elena Gallegos Picnic Area, p. 147
Foothills Trail, p. 94
Juan Tabo Cabin Trail, p. 138
La Cueva Trail, p. 89
Oso Corredor Trail, p. 33
Peak Nature Trail, p. 55
Piedra Lisa–La Luz Link, p. 88
Rozamiento Trail, p. 90
Sandia Cave Trail, p. 61
Sulphur Canyon Trail, p. 27
Tecolote Trail, p. 38

Moderate Trails:
10K Trail, p. 41
Armijo Trail, p. 24
Bart's Trail, p. 119
Boundary Loop Route, p. 133
Cañoncito Trail, p. 116
Cienega Trail, p. 22
Del Agua Route, p. 78
Ellis Trail, p. 44
Embudo Trail, p. 105
Eye of the Sandias, p. 161
Faulty Trail, p. 30
Fletcher Trail, p. 142
Hawk Watch Trail, p. 111
Juan Tabo Canyon, p. 136

Moderate Trails *(continued)*:
Mano Trail, p. 157
Movie Trail, p. 144
North Sandia Peak, p. 126
North Mystery Trail, p. 121
Osha Loop Trail, p. 47
Palomas Cliffs Trail, p. 125
Peñasco Blanco Trail, p. 57
Piedra Lisa Canyon, p. 148
Piedra Lisa Trail, p. 84
Pino Trail, p. 101
Rincon Spur Trail, p. 140
South Sandia Peak, p. 152
Strip Mine Trail, p. 76
Survey Trail, p. 131
Three Gun Spring Trail, p. 108
Tramway Trail, p. 93
Tree Spring Trail, p. 36

Difficult Trails:
Agua Sarca Route, p. 73
CCC Route, p. 113
Crest Trail, p. 64
Domingo Baca Route, p. 97
Embudito Trail, p. 102
La Luz Trail, p. 80
Ojo del Orno Route, p. 72
Osha Spring Trail, p. 62
Whitewash Trail, p. 150

Most Difficult Trail:
Chimney Canyon Route, p. 49

Appendix 3: Sandia Mountain GPS Data

Waypoint	Latitude	Longitude	Description
10KNCR	N 35° 14.257'	W 106° 26.973'	North 10K–Crest Trail junction
10KOLP	N 35° 13.932'	W 106° 26.631'	North 10K–Osha Loop Trail junction
10KTSP	N 35° 11.236'	W 106° 25.256'	South 10K–Tree Spring Trail junction
140342	N 35° 9.850'	W 106° 27.951'	Trail 140–Trail 342 junction
140AW1	N 35° 9.857'	W 106° 27.826'	Trail 140–Trail 140A junction
140TH	N 35° 9.795'	W 106° 28.200'	Parking lot and Trailhead for Trail 140
141140	N 35° 9.832'	W 106° 27.886'	Trail 141–Trail 140A junction
205END	N 35° 12.487'	W 106° 29.532'	East end of Trail 205
230341	N 35° 10.193'	W 106° 28.022'	Trail 230–Trail 341 junction
230342	N 35° 10.067'	W 106° 28.085'	Trail 230–Trail 342 junction
230365	N 35° 10.556'	W 106° 28.656'	Trail 230–Trail 365 junction
230AW1	N 35° 9.951'	W 106° 28.571'	West end of Trail 230A
230WP1	N 35° 10.610'	W 106° 28.183'	Northeast corner of Trail 230
246END	N 35° 17.064'	W 106° 27.305'	End of Trail 246
305END	N 35° 9.217'	W 106° 28.172'	Northern end of Trail 305
305TH	N 35° 8.769'	W 106° 28.404'	Southern end of Trail 305
341342	N 35° 9.695'	W 106° 27.809'	Trail 341–Trail 342 junction
342STH	N 35° 9.430'	W 106° 27.909'	Southern end of Trail 342
365AW1	N 35° 5.652'	W 106° 28.493'	Trail 365A waypoint 1
365AW2	N 35° 5.842'	W 106° 28.825'	Trail 365A waypoint 2
365H2O	N 35° 11.325'	W 106° 28.601'	Water tanks along Trail 365
365NTH	N 35° 11.423'	W 106° 28.756'	Trail 365 north trailhead (near Tram terminal)
365PWR	N 35° 5.849'	W 106° 28.339'	Trail 365 crosses power lines
365W1	N 35° 6.302'	W 106° 29.188'	Trail 365 waypoint 1
365W2	N 35° 6.567'	W 106° 29.326'	Trail 365 waypoint 2
365W3	N 35° 6.923'	W 106° 29.345'	Trail 365 waypoint 3
365W4	N 35° 7.403'	W 106° 29.349'	Trail 365 waypoint 4
365W5	N 35° 5.137'	W 106° 28.536'	Trail 365 waypoint 5
365W6	N 35° 5.521'	W 106° 28.582'	Trail 365 waypoint 6
365W7	N 35° 9.703'	W 106° 28.470'	Trail 365–Elena Gallegos road junction
365W9	N 35° 11.124'	W 106° 28.703'	Trail 365 waypoint 9
365W10	N 35° 10.860'	W 106° 28.469'	Trail 365 waypoint 10

Waypoint	Latitude	Longitude	Description
365W11	N 35° 11.215'	W 106° 28.678'	Trail 365 waypoint 11
365STH	N 35° 4.122'	W 106° 29.073'	Trail 365 south trailhead
366END	N 35° 9.214'	W 106° 28.286'	Southern end of Trail 366
445ETH	N 35° 16.943'	W 106° 28.618'	Trailhead for Trail 445E
AGSNCR	N 35° 15.771'	W 106° 27.025'	Agua Sarca–Crest Trail junction
AGSTH	N 35° 17.489'	W 106° 26.464'	Agua Sarca trailhead
AGSWP1	N 35° 17.091'	W 106° 26.630'	Agua Sarca waypoint 1
AGSWP2	N 35° 16.926'	W 106° 26.677'	Agua Sarca waypoint 2
AGSWP3	N 35° 16.562'	W 106° 26.486'	Agua Sarca waypoint 3
AGSWP4	N 35° 16.478'	W 106° 26.728'	Agua Sarca waypoint 4
ARMFLT	N 35° 9.381'	W 106° 23.336'	Armijo–Faulty Trail junction
ARMPRK	N 35° 9.902'	W 106° 22.561'	Armijo Trail parking
ARMWP1	N 35° 9.862'	W 106° 22.099'	Armijo Trail waypoint 1
BALOBS	N 35° 12.776'	W 106° 24.357'	Balsam Glade observation deck
BALTH	N 35° 12.825'	W 106° 24.489'	Balsam Glade trailhead
BNDTH	N 35° 12.159'	W 106° 30.233'	Boundary Loop trailhead/parking
BNDTR4	N 35° 13.082'	W 106° 30.032'	Boundary Loop–Trail 4 junction
BNDWP1	N 35° 12.364'	W 106° 30.128'	Boundary Loop waypoint 1
BNDWP2	N 35° 12.487'	W 106° 30.011'	Boundary Loop waypoint 2
BNDWP3	N 35° 12.468'	W 106° 30.084'	Boundary Loop waypoint 3
BNDWP4	N 35° 13.054'	W 106° 29.839'	Boundary Loop waypoint 4
BNDWP5	N 35° 12.974'	W 106° 29.977'	Boundary Loop waypoint 5
BNDWP6	N 35° 12.893'	W 106° 30.015'	Boundary Loop waypoint 6
BNDWP7	N 35° 12.738'	W 106° 30.013'	Boundary Loop waypoint 7
BNDWP8	N 35° 12.233'	W 106° 30.129'	Boundary Loop waypoint 8
BRTCNC	N 35° 8.417'	W 106° 23.171'	Bart's and Cañoncito trailheads
BRTFLT	N 35° 8.444'	W 106° 23.374'	Bart's Trail–Faulty Trail junction
BRTSCR	N 35° 8.624'	W 106° 24.837'	Bart's Trail–Crest Trail junction
BSPFLT	N 35° 10.975'	W 106° 23.307'	Bill Spring–Faulty Trail junction
BSPTH	N 35° 10.668'	W 106° 22.778'	Bill Spring trailhead
BSPWP1	N 35° 10.725'	W 106° 22.861'	Bill Spring holding tank and small spring
BSPWP2	N 35° 10.870'	W 106° 23.078'	Bill Spring
CAPSTH	N 35° 13.066'	W 106° 24.889'	Capulin Peak trailhead
CAPSW1	N 35° 13.100'	W 106° 24.884'	Capulin Peak waypoint 1 (wooden posts)
CAPSW2	N 35° 13.146'	W 106° 24.894'	Capulin Peak waypoint 2 (T in trail)
CAPSW3	N 35° 13.142'	W 106° 24.838'	Capulin Peak waypoint 3 (Y in trail)
CAPSW4	N 35° 13.206'	W 106° 24.619'	Capulin Peak waypoint 4 (dead end)
CAPSW5	N 35° 13.154'	W 106° 24.568'	Capulin Peak waypoint 5 (peak)
CCCUFL	N 35° 5.935'	W 106° 24.350'	CCC Route–Upper Faulty Trail junction
CHMLLZ	N 35° 12.761'	W 106° 28.039'	Chimney Canyon Route–La Luz Trail junction
CHMNEY	N 35° 12.795'	W 106° 27.270'	Chimney rock formation
CHMTH	N 35° 13.089'	W 106° 27.085'	Chimney Canyon trailhead

Waypoint	Latitude	Longitude	Description
CHMTH2	N 35° 12.659'	W 106° 27.000'	Chimney Canyon Route alternate trailhead
CHMWP1	N 35° 13.026'	W 106° 27.170'	Chimney Canyon Route below radio towers
CHMWP2	N 35° 12.942'	W 106° 27.240'	Chimney Canyon Route aspen grove
CHMWP3	N 35° 12.877'	W 106° 27.193'	Chimney Canyon Route along the rock slide
CIEFLT	N 35° 10.082'	W 106° 23.368'	Cienega–Faulty Trail junction
CIEHRS	N 35° 10.120'	W 106° 22.539'	Cienega Horse bypass
CIEOVL	N 35° 10.119'	W 106° 24.888'	Overlook at the top of Cienega Trail
CIESCR	N 35° 10.136'	W 106° 24.854'	Cienega–Crest Trail junction
CIETH	N 35° 10.178'	W 106° 23.047'	Cienega trailhead
CNCFLT	N 35° 8.808'	W 106° 23.343'	Cañoncito–Faulty Trail junction
CNCPK	N 35° 8.112'	W 106° 22.635'	Cañoncito parking (road blocked)
CNCSCR	N 35° 9.213'	W 106° 24.881'	Cañoncito–Crest Trail junction
CNCTRV	N 35° 8.763'	W 106° 23.234'	Travertine falls along Cañoncito Trail
COLFLT	N 35° 8.061'	W 106° 23.468'	Cole Spring–Faulty Trail junction
CRSKIW	N 35° 12.433'	W 106° 26.661'	Crest Trail–Kiwanis Cabin Trail junction
CRST3	N 35° 12.444'	W 106° 26.619'	Crest Trail–Trail 3 (cross-country) junction
CRSTNT	N 35° 12.519'	W 106° 26.879'	Crest Nature Trail
CRSTPK	N 35° 12.679'	W 106° 26.958'	Crest parking lot
CRSTRM	N 35° 11.822'	W 106° 26.089'	Crest Trail (130)–Tram trailhead
CSPLLZ	N 35° 12.276'	W 106° 26.849'	Crest Spur–La Luz Trail junction
CSPSW1	N 35° 12.577'	W 106° 26.994'	Crest Spur Trail first switchback
CSPTH	N 35° 12.570'	W 106° 26.921'	Crest Spur (north) trailhead
CSPWP1	N 35° 12.442'	W 106° 26.921'	Crest Spur stairs
CUPARK	N 35° 4.752'	W 106° 29.068'	Parking at east end of Copper Blvd.
DAGPLS	N 35° 15.755'	W 106° 28.079'	Del Agua–Piedra Lisa Trail junction
DAGTH	N 35° 16.613'	W 106° 29.050'	Del Agua Trailhead
DAGWP1	N 35° 16.232'	W 106° 28.992'	Del Agua waypoint 1
DAGWP2	N 35° 16.094'	W 106° 28.791'	Del Agua waypoint 2
DAGWP3	N 35° 15.835'	W 106° 28.303'	Del Agua waypoint 3
DBCFRK	N 35° 10.692'	W 106° 27.982'	Fork in Domingo Baca Trail
DBCTH	N 35° 10.262'	W 106° 28.011'	Trailhead to Domingo Baca Route
DBCWP1	N 35° 10.520'	W 106° 28.117'	Domingo Baca waypoint 1
DBCWP2	N 35° 10.805'	W 106° 27.718'	Domingo Baca waypoint 2
DBCWP3	N 35° 10.886'	W 106° 27.594'	Domingo Baca waypoint 3
DBCWP4	N 35° 10.882'	W 106° 27.442'	Domingo Baca waypoint 4
DDUCK	N 35° 12.323'	W 106° 27.039'	Donald Duck Rock visible from La Luz Trail
DORNCR	N 35° 16.890'	W 106° 26.097'	Del Orno Route–Crest Trail upper junction
DORTH	N 35° 17.451'	W 106° 26.323'	Del Orno Route lower trailhead
DORWP1	N 35° 17.068'	W 106° 26.154'	Del Orno waypoint 1

Waypoint	Latitude	Longitude	Description
EBTORD	N 35° 8.221'	W 106° 28.725'	Oso Ridge Trail turnoff from Embudito Trail
EBTOTH	N 35° 8.182'	W 106° 28.910'	Embudito Trailhead
EBTPLT	N 35° 8.062'	W 106° 28.423'	Embudito Trail plateau where trail splits
EBTWP1	N 35° 8.031'	W 106° 28.030'	Embudito Trail waypoint 1
EBTWP2	N 35° 8.029'	W 106° 28.000'	Embudito Trail waypoint 2
EBTWP3	N 35° 8.028'	W 106° 27.477'	Embudito Trail waypoint 3
EBTWP4	N 35° 6.799'	W 106° 25.830'	Embudito Trail waypoint 4
EBTWP5	N 35° 7.234'	W 106° 25.856'	Embudito Trail waypoint 5
EBTWP6	N 35° 6.706'	W 106° 25.704'	Embudito Trail waypoint 6
ECAVE	N 35° 12.250'	W 106° 24.873'	Embudo Cave
ECAVE1	N 35° 12.068'	W 106° 24.587'	Embudo Cave trailhead
ECAVE2	N 35° 12.072'	W 106° 24.656'	Embudo Cave waypoint 2
ECAVE3	N 35° 12.198'	W 106° 24.736'	Embudo Cave waypoint 3
EGPK	N 35° 9.704'	W 106° 28.191'	Elena Gallegos parking lot
ELI10K	N 35° 14.057'	W 106° 26.852'	Ellis–10K Trail junction
ELIEND	N 35° 14.967'	W 106° 27.017'	Ellis Trail north end
ELIOLP	N 35° 14.692'	W 106° 26.990'	Ellis–Osha Loop Trail junction
ELIPWR	N 35° 13.007'	W 106° 26.729'	Ellis Trail power lines
ELISPK	N 35° 12.543'	W 106° 26.458'	Ellis Trail parking
EMB365	N 35° 5.944'	W 106° 28.298'	Embudo –Trail 365 junction
EMBPOS	N 35° 5.990'	W 106° 26.735'	Embudo–Post Pass Trail junction
EMBSPR	N 35° 5.804'	W 106° 27.817'	Embudo Spring
EMBTGS	N 35° 6.206'	W 106° 26.556'	Embudo–Three Gun Spring Trail junction
EMBWP1	N 35° 5.800'	W 106° 27.879'	Embudo Trail waypoint 1
EMBWP2	N 35° 5.772'	W 106° 27.572'	Embudo Trail waypoint 2
EMBWP3	N 35° 5.761'	W 106° 27.556'	Embudo Trail waypoint 3
EMBWP4	N 35° 6.090'	W 106° 26.879'	Embudo Trail waypoint 4
EYEWP1	N 35° 4.303'	W 106° 28.936'	Eye of the Sandias waypoint 1
EYEWP2	N 35° 4.304'	W 106° 28.823'	Eye of the Sandias waypoint 2
EYEWP3	N 35° 4.366'	W 106° 28.167'	Eye of the Sandias waypoint 3
EYEWP4	N 35° 4.374'	W 106° 28.209'	Eye of the Sandias waypoint 4
EYEWP5	N 35° 4.785'	W 106° 28.717'	Eye of the Sandias waypoint 5
EYEWP6	N 35° 4.812'	W 106° 28.725'	Eye of the Sandias waypoint 6
FLETH	N 35° 13.851'	W 106° 28.774'	Fletcher trailhead
FLEWP1	N 35° 13.877'	W 106° 28.714'	Fletcher Trail waypoint 1
FLEWP2	N 35° 14.191'	W 106° 28.479'	Fletcher Trail waypoint 2
FLEWP3	N 35° 14.083'	W 106° 28.636'	Fletcher Trail waypoint 3
FLEWP4	N 35° 14.215'	W 106° 28.274'	Fletcher Trail waypoint 4
FLEWP5	N 35° 14.093'	W 106° 28.090'	Fletcher Trail waypoint 5 (UNM Spire)
FLEWP6	N 35° 14.087'	W 106° 28.017'	Fletcher Trail waypoint 6
FLTOSO	N 35° 10.863'	W 106° 23.276'	Faulty–Oso Corredor Trail junction
FLTSUL	N 35° 10.371'	W 106° 23.222'	Faulty –Sulphur Canyon Trail junction
FLTTHG	N 35° 8.813'	W 106° 23.319'	Thong tree aside Faulty Trail

Waypoint	Latitude	Longitude	Description
FLTWP1	N 35° 7.530'	W 106° 23.620'	Faulty–unknown trail junction
FLTWP2	N 35° 10.095'	W 106° 23.256'	Faulty Trail waypoint 2
FLTWP3	N 35° 10.316'	W 106° 23.180'	Horse bypass from Faulty Trail
FORPK1	N 35° 7.344'	W 106° 23.878'	Forest Park–Faulty Trail junction
FORPK2	N 35° 6.991'	W 106° 22.981'	East end of Forest Park Trail
GRAWP1	N 35° 11.845'	W 106° 26.064'	Gravel Pit Trail south terminus
HWKTH	N 35° 4.959'	W 106° 26.618'	Hawk Watch trailhead
HWKWP1	N 35° 5.229'	W 106° 25.949'	Hawk Watch plateau
HWKWP2	N 35° 5.314'	W 106° 25.753'	Hawk Watch waypoint 2
INSCPK	N 35° 5.943'	W 106° 28.800'	Parking lot at end of Indian School
JARCAB	N 35° 12.025'	W 106° 28.995'	Jaral Cabin
JTBCAB	N 35° 12.359'	W 106° 29.800'	Juan Tabo Cabin
JTBWP1	N 35° 12.356'	W 106° 29.913'	Juan Tabo Cabin alternate parking
KIWCAB	N 35° 12.206'	W 106° 26.594'	Kiwanis Cabin
LCVTH	N 35° 12.267'	W 106° 29.232'	La Cueva Trail trailhead
LL137B	N 35° 12.747'	W 106° 28.217'	La Luz–Trail 137B junction
LLZRK1	N 35° 12.308'	W 106° 26.884'	La Luz top of rock slides
LLZRK2	N 35° 12.437'	W 106° 27.313'	La Luz bottom of rock slides
LLZTH	N 35° 13.181'	W 106° 28.850'	La Luz trailhead/parking lot
LLZTRM	N 35° 12.817'	W 106° 28.535'	La Luz–Tramway Trail junction
LNDMIN	N 35° 14.728'	W 106° 25.940'	Landsend barite mine
LNDMRK	N 35° 14.710'	W 106° 25.833'	Landsend barite stone marker
MEDSPR	N 35° 13.938'	W 106° 26.546'	Media Spring
MENLPK	N 35° 6.301'	W 106° 29.300'	Menaul parking
MNONTH	N 35° 5.525'	W 106° 28.344'	Mano northern trailhead
MNOSDL	N 35° 4.803'	W 106° 27.756'	Mano Trail saddlepoint
MNOSTH	N 35° 5.019'	W 106° 28.593'	Mano southern trailhead
MNOWP1	N 35° 5.486'	W 106° 28.220'	Mano Trail waypoint 1
MNOWP2	N 35° 5.431'	W 106° 28.157'	Mano Trail waypoint 2
MNOWP3	N 35° 5.345'	W 106° 28.020'	Mano Trail waypoint 3
MNOWP4	N 35° 5.223'	W 106° 27.995'	Mano Trail waypoint 4
MNOWP5	N 35° 5.145'	W 106° 27.961'	Mano Trail waypoint 5
MNOWP6	N 35° 5.016'	W 106° 27.988'	Mano Trail waypoint 6
MNOWP7	N 35° 4.930'	W 106° 27.978'	Mano Trail waypoint 7
MNOWP8	N 35° 4.890'	W 106° 27.984'	Mano Trail waypoint 8
MOVPLS	N 35° 13.849'	W 106° 28.772'	Movie Trail–Piedra Lisa Trail junction
MOVWP1	N 35° 13.841'	W 106° 28.606'	Movie Trail waypoint 1
MOVWP2	N 35° 13.916'	W 106° 28.388'	Movie Trail waypoint 2
MOVWP3	N 35° 13.976'	W 106° 28.248'	Movie Trail waypoint 3
N10KPK	N 35° 12.595'	W 106° 26.161'	North 10K parking lot
N10KPW	N 35° 13.034'	W 106° 26.472'	North 10K power lines
NCROLP	N 35° 14.472'	W 106° 27.032'	Crest Trail–Osha Loop Trail junction
NCRPBL	N 35° 15.759'	W 106° 26.460'	Crest Trail–Peñasco Blanco Trail junction
NCRPWR	N 35° 12.988'	W 106° 27.038'	Crest Trail power lines

Waypoint	Latitude	Longitude	Description
NCRSTR	N 35° 15.636'	W 106° 26.919'	Crest Trail crosses streambed
NCRTH	N 35° 17.487'	W 106° 26.372'	Crest Trail trailhead (Tunnel Spring)
NMYPRK	N 35° 10.876'	W 106° 22.620'	North Mystery Trail south parking area
NMYST1	N 35° 11.189'	W 106° 22.828'	North Mystery Trail waypoint 1
NMYST2	N 35° 12.438'	W 106° 23.277'	North Mystery Trail at saddle point
NMYST3	N 35° 12.786'	W 106° 23.197'	North Mystery Trail at power lines
NMYST4	N 35° 12.920'	W 106° 23.268'	North Mystery Trail bottom of Madera Canyon
NMYST5	N 35° 13.631'	W 106° 23.969'	North Mystery Trail enters Lagunita Seca
NMYST6	N 35° 13.675'	W 106° 24.057'	North Mystery Trail waypoint 6
NPKOL1	N 35° 13.486'	W 106° 27.136'	South turn-off to overlook from Crest Trail
NPKOL2	N 35° 13.646'	W 106° 27.123'	North turn-off to overlook from Crest Trail
NPKWP1	N 35° 13.791'	W 106° 27.145'	North Sandia Peak route waypoint 1
NPKWP2	N 35° 13.817'	W 106° 27.168'	North Sandia Peak route waypoint 2
NRTHPK	N 35° 14.108'	W 106° 27.401'	North Sandia Peak
OLPOSP	N 35° 14.569'	W 106° 26.193'	Osha Loop–Osha Spring Trail junction
OLPSB1	N 35° 14.564'	W 106° 26.749'	Osha Loop switchback 1
OLPSB2	N 35° 14.791'	W 106° 26.776'	Osha Loop switchback 2
OLPWP1	N 35° 13.984'	W 106° 26.539'	Osha Loop canyon overlook
ORDWP1	N 35° 8.225'	W 106° 28.769'	Oso Ridge Trail waypoint 1
ORDWP2	N 35° 8.171'	W 106° 27.635'	Oso Ridge Trail waypoint 2
ORDWP3	N 35° 8.251'	W 106° 27.426'	Oso Ridge Trail waypoint 3
OSOPSS	N 35° 7.065'	W 106° 26.596'	Oso Pass
OSOTSP	N 35° 11.524'	W 106° 24.501'	Oso Corredor–Tree Spring Trail junction
OSPPBL	N 35° 14.664'	W 106° 26.129'	Osha Spring Trail–Peñasco Blanco Trail junction
OSPSW	N 35° 16.737'	W 106° 24.672'	Osha Spring Trail switchback
OSPTH	N 35° 16.516'	W 106° 24.555'	Osha Spring Trail trailhead
OSPWP1	N 35° 16.295'	W 106° 24.824'	Osha Spring Trail waypoint 1
OSPWP2	N 35° 15.759'	W 106° 25.190'	Osha Spring Trail waypoint 2
OSPWP3	N 35° 14.691'	W 106° 25.794'	Osha Spring Trail waypoint 3
OSPWP4	N 35° 14.677'	W 106° 26.059'	Osha Spring Trail waypoint 4
PBLWP1	N 35° 14.815'	W 106° 26.191'	Peñasco Blanco waypoint 1
PBLWP2	N 35° 14.779'	W 106° 26.187'	Peñasco Blanco waypoint 2
PBLWP3	N 35° 14.732'	W 106° 26.203'	Peñasco Blanco waypoint 3
PLCWP1	N 35° 6.678'	W 106° 29.025'	Piedra Lisa Canyon waypoint 1
PLCWP2	N 35° 6.928'	W 106° 28.833'	Piedra Lisa Canyon waypoint 2
PLCWP3	N 35° 6.938'	W 106° 28.788'	Piedra Lisa Canyon waypoint 3
PLCWP4	N 35° 6.873'	W 106° 28.710'	Piedra Lisa Canyon waypoint 4
PLCWP5	N 35° 6.824'	W 106° 28.457'	Piedra Lisa Canyon waypoint 5

Waypoint	Latitude	Longitude	Description
PLCYPK	N 35° 6.739'	W 106° 29.286'	Piedra Lisa Canyon parking
PLLLZ1	N 35° 13.393'	W 106° 28.996'	Piedra Lisa–La Luz Link northwest trailhead
PLLLZ2	N 35° 13.296'	W 106° 28.824'	Piedra Lisa–La Luz Link waypoint 1
PLLLZ3	N 35° 13.215'	W 106° 28.758'	Piedra Lisa–La Luz Link waypoint 2
PLPKEN	N 35° 14.081'	W 106° 24.386'	Palomas Cliffs Trail end
PLPKSW	N 35° 13.622'	W 106° 24.091'	Palomas Cliffs Trail switchback
PLPKTH	N 35° 13.584'	W 106° 24.561'	Palomas Cliffs trailhead
PLSTHN	N 35° 16.734'	W 106° 28.711'	Piedra Lisa (north) trailhead
PLSTHS	N 35° 13.378'	W 106° 29.005'	Piedra Lisa (south) trailhead
PLSWP1	N 35° 14.676'	W 106° 28.510'	Piedra Lisa Trail crosses the Rincon
PLSWP2	N 35° 15.193'	W 106° 28.371'	Piedra Lisa waypoint 2
PLSWP3	N 35° 16.593'	W 106° 28.483'	Piedra Lisa waypoint 3
PLSWP4	N 35° 13.698'	W 106° 28.938'	Piedra Lisa waypoint 4
PNOSCR	N 35° 10.144'	W 106° 24.850'	Pino Trail–Crest Trail junction
PNOSPR	N 35° 10.102'	W 106° 25.487'	Pino Spring
PNOWP1	N 35° 9.907'	W 106° 27.415'	Pino Trail crosses Forest Service boundary
POSTPS	N 35° 5.744'	W 106° 26.819'	Post Pass (approximate location)
PROW	N 35° 13.931'	W 106° 28.055'	Prow rock formation
REDSDL	N 35° 6.992'	W 106° 23.830'	Saddle point east of Red Hill (Faulty Trail)
ROZPK	N 35° 11.829'	W 106° 29.420'	Rozamiento parking
ROZTRM	N 35° 11.998'	W 106° 28.946'	Rozamiento–Tramway Trail junction
ROZW1	N 35° 11.990'	W 106° 29.074'	Rozamiento waypoint 1
RPTWP1	N 35° 11.952'	W 106° 26.082'	Rocky Point Trail north terminus
RPTWP2	N 35° 12.429'	W 106° 26.409'	Rocky Point Trail south terminus
RSPWP1	N 35° 14.599'	W 106° 28.445'	Rincon Spur Trail waypoint 1
RSPWP2	N 35° 14.624'	W 106° 28.300'	Rincon Spur Trail waypoint 2
RSPWP3	N 35° 14.614'	W 106° 28.188'	Rincon Spur Trail waypoint 3
RSPWP4	N 35° 14.601'	W 106° 28.106'	Rincon Spur Trail waypoint 4
RSPWP5	N 35° 14.830'	W 106° 28.733'	Rincon Spur Trail waypoint 5
S10KPK	N 35° 12.552'	W 106° 26.129'	South 10K parking lot
S10KSK	N 35° 12.084'	W 106° 25.834'	South 10K northernmost ski run
S10KW1	N 35° 11.838'	W 106° 25.598'	South 10K third chair lift
S10KW2	N 35° 11.771'	W 106° 25.551'	South 10K southernmost ski run
SCNCRS	N 35° 13.488'	W 106° 25.119'	Sandia Conference Center "old cross"
SCNFCT	N 35° 13.578'	W 106° 25.109'	Sandia Conference Center
SCRCCC	N 35° 6.711'	W 106° 25.612'	Crest Trail–CCC Route junction
SCREBT	N 35° 6.666'	W 106° 25.627'	Crest Trail–Embudito Trail junction
SCRLFL	N 35° 5.849'	W 106° 23.832'	Crest Trail–Lower Faulty Trail junction
SCRRDG	N 35° 5.687'	W 106° 25.694'	Crest Trail ridgeline
SCRSPK	N 35° 5.373'	W 106° 23.494'	(south) Crest Trail parking area
SCRSPR	N 35° 5.965'	W 106° 25.545'	Crest Trail–South Sandia Spring
SCRTRV	N 35° 5.696'	W 106° 23.573'	Crest Trail–Travertine Falls
SCRUFL	N 35° 5.916'	W 106° 24.360'	Crest Trail–Upper Faulty Trail junction

Waypoint	Latitude	Longitude	Description
SCRW1	N 35° 5.707'	W 106° 25.484'	Crest Trail waypoint 1
SCRW2	N 35° 5.571'	W 106° 25.635'	Crest Trail waypoint 2
SCRW3	N 35° 7.307'	W 106° 25.669'	Crest Trail waypoint 3
SCRW4	N 35° 7.935'	W 106° 25.266'	Crest Trail waypoint 4
SCRW5	N 35° 11.448'	W 106° 25.741'	Crest Trail switchback
SCRW6	N 35° 11.592'	W 106° 25.805'	Crest Trail switchback
SHLDKE	N 35° 14.191'	W 106° 27.689'	Knife Edge of the Shield
SMLEND	N 35° 11.952'	W 106° 22.565'	Smelter Trail end
SMLSPT	N 35° 11.266'	W 106° 22.673'	Smelter Trail saddle point
SNDCV1	N 35° 15.016'	W 106° 24.588'	Sandia Cave trailhead
SNDCV2	N 35° 15.282'	W 106° 24.336'	Sandia Cave (trail end)
SPEAK1	N 35° 6.984'	W 106° 25.683'	Crest Trail cut-off to South Peak
SPEAK2	N 35° 7.009'	W 106° 25.740'	Waypoint 2 from Crest Trail to South Peak
SPEAK3	N 35° 7.026'	W 106° 25.870'	Waypoint 3 from Crest Trail to South Peak
SRV10K	N 35° 14.140'	W 106° 26.948'	Survey–10K Trail junction
SRVOLP	N 35° 14.537'	W 106° 27.013'	Survey–Osha Loop Trail junction
SRVPWR	N 35° 13.006'	W 106° 26.865'	Survey power line
SRVSWT	N 35° 12.583'	W 106° 26.639'	Survey–Switchback Trail junction
SRVTH	N 35° 12.727'	W 106° 26.763'	Survey trailhead
SRVWP1	N 35° 12.508'	W 106° 26.548'	Survey Trail waypoint 1
SRVWP2	N 35° 12.471'	W 106° 26.478'	Survey Trail south terminus
STHPK	N 35° 7.235'	W 106° 25.842'	South Peak
STR246	N 35° 17.725'	W 106° 27.418'	Strip Mine Trail–Trail 246 junction
STREND	N 35° 17.866'	W 106° 27.386'	Strip Mine Trail east end
STRTH	N 35° 18.018'	W 106° 28.837'	Strip Mine (west) trailhead
SULPK	N 35° 10.339'	W 106° 22.587'	Sulphur Canyon parking lot
SULSPR	N 35° 10.375'	W 106° 22.612'	Sulphur Spring
SULTH	N 35° 10.461'	W 106° 22.901'	Sulphur Canyon trailhead
SWBT94	N 35° 12.529'	W 106° 26.850'	Switchback Trail–Trail 94 junction
T2BTR4	N 35° 13.220'	W 106° 29.921'	Trail 2B–Trail 4 junction
T2BWP1	N 35° 13.334'	W 106° 29.710'	Trail 2B waypoint 1
T2BWP2	N 35° 13.282'	W 106° 29.851'	Trail 2B waypoint 2
T94TH	N 35° 12.564'	W 106° 26.878'	Trail 94 (northern) trailhead
TECLP	N 35° 11.691'	W 106° 23.785'	Tecolote Trail loop
TECMIN	N 35° 11.998'	W 106° 24.111'	Tecolote Trail mine opening
TECTH	N 35° 12.036'	W 106° 24.299'	Tecolote trailhead
TGSTH	N 35° 4.587'	W 106° 26.649'	Three Gun Spring trailhead
TGSWP1	N 35° 4.960'	W 106° 26.617'	Three Gun Spring Trail wilderness boundary
TGSWP2	N 35° 5.808'	W 106° 26.428'	Three Gun Spring Trail switchbacks
THEEYE	N 35° 4.577'	W 106° 27.989'	Eye of the Sandias
TORRSP	N 35° 9.406'	W 106° 23.599'	Torro Spring
TR2T2B	N 35° 13.312'	W 106° 29.443'	Trail 2–Trail 2B junction
TR2TH	N 35° 13.007'	W 106° 29.245'	Trail 2 trailhead / parking

Waypoint	Latitude	Longitude	Description
TR2WP1	N 35° 13.323'	W 106° 29.423'	Trail 2 waypoint 1
TR2WP2	N 35° 13.555'	W 106° 29.308'	Trail 2 waypoint 2 (end)
TR4WP1	N 35° 12.947'	W 106° 30.173'	Trail 4 boundary with Sandia Pueblo
TR4WP2	N 35° 13.933'	W 106° 29.436'	Trail 4 north terminus
TREESP	N 35° 11.614'	W 106° 24.173'	Tree Spring
TRM137	N 35° 12.786'	W 106° 28.660'	Tramway Trail–Trail 137 B junction
TRMLCN	N 35° 12.379'	W 106° 28.917'	Tramway Trail entrance to La Cueva Canyon
TRMLCV	N 35° 12.333'	W 106° 29.016'	Tramway Trail turn-off to La Cueva Picnic Grounds
TRMPK	N 35° 11.519'	W 106° 28.753'	Tramway Trail parking lot (south trailhead)
TRMWP1	N 35° 11.945'	W 106° 29.027'	Tramway Trail three signposts
TSPTH	N 35° 11.632'	W 106° 24.287'	Tree Spring trailhead
TWA	N 35° 11.696'	W 106° 26.552'	TWA Crash Site
TWAWP1	N 35° 11.820'	W 106° 26.538'	Waypoint 1 above TWA wreckage
TWAWP2	N 35° 11.954'	W 106° 26.538'	Waypoint 2 above TWA wreckage
TWAWP3	N 35° 12.085'	W 106° 26.470'	Waypoint 3 above TWA wreckage
UFLLFL	N 35° 6.717'	W 106° 23.876'	Upper Faulty–Lower Faulty Trail junction
WHWWP1	N 35° 7.019'	W 106° 27.924'	Whitewash Trail waypoint 1
WHWWP2	N 35° 6.980'	W 106° 28.067'	Whitewash Trail waypoint 2
WHWWP3	N 35° 6.836'	W 106° 28.109'	Whitewash Trail waypoint 3
WLFDOC	N 35° 10.527'	W 106° 22.661'	Wolf Spring trailhead in Doc Long Picnic Grounds
WLFSUL	N 35° 10.397'	W 106° 22.636'	Wolf Spring trailhead in Sulphur Canyon Picnic Grounds

Appendix 4: Additional Reading

Beard, Sam. *Ski Touring in Northern New Mexico.* Albuquerque: Nordic Press, 1989.

Bennett, Sarah. *The Mountain Biker's Guide to New Mexico.* Birmingham, AL: Menasha Ridge Press, 1994.

Blouin, Nicole. *Mountain Biking Albuquerque.* Helena, MT: Falcon Publishing, 1999.

Darvill, Fred T. Jr. *Mountaineering Medicine and Backcountry Medical Guide.* Berkeley: Wilderness Press, 1998.

Elmore, Francis H. *Shrubs and Trees of the Southwest Uplands.* Tucson: Southwest Parks and Monuments Association, 1976.

Fischer, Pierre C. *Seventy Common Cacti of the Southwest.* Tucson: Southwest Parks and Monuments Association, 1989.

Hill, Mike. *Hikers and Climbers Guide to the Sandias.* 3rd ed. Albuquerque: University of New Mexico Press, 1993.

Julyan, Robert. *New Mexico Wilderness Areas.* Englewood, CO: Westercliffe Publishers, 1998.

———. *The Place Names of New Mexico.* Albuquerque: University of New Mexico Press, 1996.

Julyan, Robert, and Mary Stuever, eds. *Field Guide to the Sandia Mountains.* Albuquerque: University of New Mexico Press, 2005.

Kelley, Vincent C. and Stuart A. Northrop. *Geology of the Sandia Mountains and Vicinity, New Mexico.* Socorro, NM: New Mexico Bureau of Mines and Resources, 1975.

Maurer, Steven G. *Sandia Mountain Visitors Guide.* Albuquerque: Southwest Natural and Cultural Heritage Association, 1994.

McGivney, Annette. *Leave No Trace.* Seattle: The Mountaineers, 1998.

Pierce, J. Rush and Amanda Pierce. *Mountain Wildflowers of Northern New Mexico.* Granbury, TX: JRP Publications, 2001.

Stackey, Martha, and George Palmer. *Western Trees: A Field Guide.* Helena, MT: Falcon Publishing, 1998.

Van Tilburg, C., ed. *First Aid: A Pocket Guide.* Seattle: The Mountaineers, 1982.

Index